The Bird Study Book

by Thomas Gilbert

TO MY WIFE

ELSIE WEATHERLY PEARSON

PREFACE

This book has been written for the consideration of that ever-increasing class of Americans who are interested in acquiring a greater familiarity with the habits and activities of wild birds. There are many valuable publications treating more or less exhaustively of the classification of birds, as well as of form, colour, distribution, migration, songs, and foods. Here an attempt is made to place before the reader a brief consideration of these and many similar topics, and suggest lines of action and thought that may perhaps stimulate a fuller study of the subject. Attention is also given to the relation of birds to mankind and the effect of civilisation on the bird-life of the country. The book is not intended so much for the advanced student in ornithology, as for the beginner. Its purpose is to answer many of the questions that students in this charming field of outdoor study are constantly asking of those more advanced in bird-lore. In conformity with the custom employed during many years of college and summer-school teaching, the author has discussed numerous details of field observation, the importance of which is so often overlooked by writers on the subject.

If one can, in the recounting of some experience that he has found interesting, awaken in the mind of a sympathetic hearer a desire to go forth and acquire a similar experience, then indeed may he regard himself as a worthy disciple of the immortal Pestalozzi. Let the teacher who would instruct pupils in bird-study first acquire, therefore, that love for the subject which is sure to come when one begins to learn the birds and observe their movements. This book, it is hoped, will aid such seekers after truth by the simple means of pointing out some of the interesting things that may be sought and readily found in the field and by the open road.

In the preparation of this volume much valuable aid has been received from Messrs. E. W. Nelson, F. E. L. Beal, Wells W. Cooke, T. S. Palmer, H. C. Oberholser, and others of the United States Biological Survey, for which the author desires to make grateful acknowledgment.

Parts of some of the chapters have previously appeared in the "Craftsman Magazine" and "Country Life in America," and are here reproduced by the courtesy of the editors.

T. GILBERT PEARSON.

CONTENTS

CHAPTER

Caution in Nest Hunting--Going Afield--Notebooks--Reporting Blanks--Bird Books--Movements of Birds--Artificial Cover in Hiding--The Umbrella Blind--Conclusion.

Nest Hunting--Behaviour when Nest Is Discovered--Lessons to Be Learned--Character of Material Used--Nests in Holes--Variety of Locations--Variation in Families--Meagre Nests.

Parental Care of Young--Sharing the Labours--Length of Mated Life--A Much-married Bluebird--The Faithful Canada Geese--Unmated Birds--Polygamy Among Birds--The Outcast.

Moulting--Why Birds Migrate--The Gathering Flocks--The Usual Movement--The Travelling Shore Birds--The World's Migrating Champion--Perils of Migration--Keeping Migration Records.

A Good Time for Field Walks--The Downy's Winter Quarters--Birds and the Night--The Food Question in Winter--When the Food Supply Fails--Wild Fowl Destroyed in the Oil Fields--Hunting Winter Birds.

A Government Report--Plagues of Insects--Some Useful Birds--The Question of the Weed Seeds--Dealing with the Rodent Pests--The Terror That Flies by Night--A Seldom Recognised Blessing.

Number of Birds in the World--Number in the Different States--Increase of Farm-land Species--Effect of Forest Devastation--Commercializing Birds--Wild Pigeon--Ivory-billed Woodpecker--Labrador Duck--Great Auk--Eskimo Curlew.

War on the Sea Swallows--What the Ladies Wore--The Story of the Egrets--Amateur Feather Hunters--Maribou--Pheasants--Numidie--Goura--Women's Love for Feathers--Ostrich Feathers Are Desirable.

Definition of Game--Audubon Laws--Game Law Enforcement--Lacy Lava--Federal Migratory Bird Law--History of Game Laws--The Theory of Shiras--Work of the Bird Committee--Government Explanations--World's Only Bird Treaty.

First Federal Bird Reservation--Congressional Sanction--Florida Reservations--Distant Reservations--President Taft a Bird Protectionist--Audubon Society Reservations--The Corkscrew Rookery--Wardens Shot by Plume Hunters.

Natural Nesting Places Destroyed--Nesting Boxes for Birds--Some Rules for Making and Erecting Bird Boxes--Sites of Bird Boxes--Feeding Birds--Community Sanctuaries--Birdcraft Sanctuary--Cemeteries as Bird Sanctuaries--A Birdless Cemetery--Birds of a New York Graveyard--Enemies to Be Eliminated--Berries and Fruit for Birds.

THE BIRD STUDY BOOK

CHAPTER I

FIRST ACQUAINTANCE WITH THE BIRDS

It is in spring that wild birds make their strongest appeal to the human mind; in fact, the words "birds" and "spring" seem almost synonymous, so accustomed are we to associate one with the other. All the wild riotous singing, all the brave flashing of wings and tail, all the mad dashing in and out among the thickets or soaring upward above the tree-tops, are impelled by the perfectly natural instinct of mating and rearing young. And where, pray, dwells the soul so poor that it does not thrill in response to the appeals of the ardent lover, even if it be a bird, or feel sympathy upon beholding expressions of parental love and solicitude. Most people, therefore, are interested in such spring bird life as comes to their notice, the extent of this interest depending {4} in part on their opportunity for observation, but more especially, perhaps, on their individual taste and liking for things out of doors.

It would seem safe to assume that there is hardly any one who does not know by sight at least a few birds. Nearly every one in the eastern United States and Canada knows the Robin, Crow, and English Sparrow; in the South most people are acquainted with the Mockingbird and Turkey Buzzard; in California the House Finch is abundant about the towns and cities; and to the dwellers in the Prairie States the Meadowlark is very familiar.

Taking such knowledge, however slight, as a basis, there is no reason why any one, if he so desires, should not, with a little effort, get on neighbourly terms with a large number of birds of the region, and spring is a most favourable time to begin such an effort. One may learn more about a bird's habits by closely observing its movements for a few hours at this season than by watching it for a month later on. The life that centres about the nest is most {5} absorbing. Few sights are more stimulating to interest in outdoor life than spying on a pair of wild birds engaged in nest building. Nest hunting, therefore, soon becomes a part of the bird student's occupation, and I heartily recommend such a course to beginners, provided great care is exercised not to injure the nests and their contents.

Caution in Nest Hunting.--A thoughtful person will, of course, be careful in approaching a wild bird's nest, otherwise much mischief may be done in a very short time. I have known "dainty eggs" and "darling baby-birds" to be literally visited to death by well-meaning people, with the best of intentions. The parents become discouraged by constantly recurring alarms and desert the nest, or a cat will follow the path made through the weeds and leave nothing in the nest worth observing. Even the bending of limbs, or the pushing aside of leaves, will produce a change in the surroundings, which, however slight, may be sufficient to draw the attention of some feathered enemy.

When one stumbles on the nest of a Quail, Meadowlark, or Oven-bird, it is well not to approach it closely, because all over the country many night-prowling animals have the habit of following by scent the footsteps of any one who has lately gone along through the woods or across the fields. One afternoon by the rarest chance I found three Quails' nests containing eggs. The next morning I took out a friend to share the pleasure of my discoveries. We found every nest destroyed and the eggs eaten. My trail the evening before lay through cultivated fields, and it was thus easy for us to find in the soft ground the tracks of the fox or small dog that, during the night, had followed the trail with calamitous results to the birds. When finding the nests I had made the mistake of going to within a few inches of them. Had I stopped six feet away the despoiler that followed probably never would have known there was a nest near, for unless a dog approaches within a very few feet of a brooding Quail it seems not to possess the power of smelling it.

Going Afield.--It is rarely necessary to go far afield to begin the study of birds. Often one may get good views of birds from one's open window, as many species build their nests close to the house when the surroundings are favourable. Last spring {8} I counted eighteen kinds of birds one morning while sitting on the veranda of a friend's house, and later found the nests of no less than seven of them within sight of the house. When one starts out to hunt birds it is well to bear in mind a few simple rules. The first of these is to go quietly. One's good sense would of course tell him not to rush headlong through the woods, talking loudly to a companion, stepping upon brittle twigs, and crashing through the underbrush. Go quietly, stopping to listen every few steps. Make no violent motions, as such actions often frighten a bird more than a noise. Do not wear brightly coloured clothing, but garments of neutral tones which blend well with the surroundings of field and wood. It is a good idea to sit silently for a time on some log or stump, and soon the birds will come about you, for they seldom notice a person who is motionless. A great aid to field study is a good Field Glass. A glass enables one to see the colours of small birds hopping about the shrubbery, or moving through the branches of trees. With its {9} aid one may learn much of their movements, and even observe the kind of food they consume. A very serviceable glass may be secured at a price varying from five to ten dollars. The National Association of Audubon Societies, New York City, sells a popular one for five dollars. If you choose a more expensive, high-powered binocular, it will be found of greater advantage when watching birds at a distance, as on a lake or at the seashore.

Notebooks.--The bird student should early acquire the custom of making notes on such subjects as are of special interest. In listening to the song or call of some unknown bird, the notes can usually be written down in characters of human speech so that they may be recalled later with sufficient accuracy to identify the singer. It is well to keep a list of the species observed when on a trip. For many years in my field excursions I have kept careful lists of the birds seen and identified, and have found these notes to be of subsequent use and pleasure. In college and summer-school work I {10} have always insisted on pupils cultivating the notebook habit, and results have well justified this course.

In making notes on a bird that you do not know it is well to state the size by comparing it with some bird you know, as, for example, "smaller than an English Sparrow," "about the size of a Robin," and so on. Try to determine the true colours of the birds and record these. Also note the shape and approximate length of the bill. This, for example, may be short and conical like a Canary's, awl-shaped like the bill of a Warbler, or very long and slender like that of a Snipe. By failing to observe these simple rules the learner may be in despair when he tries to find out the name of his strange bird by examining a bird book, or may cause some kindly friend an equal amount of annoyance.

As a further aid to subsequent identification it is well to record the place where the bird was seen, for example: "hopping up the side of a tree," "wading in a marsh," "circling about in the air," or "feeding {12} on dandelions." Such secondary information, while often a valuable aid to identification, would in itself hardly be sufficient to enable an ornithologist to render the service desired.

That a young correspondent of mine entertained a contrary view was evident from a letter I received a few weeks ago from an inexperienced boy enthusiast, who was a member of a newly formed nature-study class. Here is the exact wording of the communication: "Dear Sir: 10 A. M. Wind East. Cloudy. Small bird seen on ground in orchard. Please name. P. S. All the leaves have fallen."

Reporting Blanks.--A convenient booklet of reporting blanks and directions for using them is issued by the National Association of Audubon Societies, New York City. This is very useful in recording descriptions of birds. (See sample, page 13.) The blanks may be sent to the office of the National Association and the species described will be named.

Bird Books.--There are a number of inexpensive {14} books which contain illustrations of birds in natural colours. One of these will be of the greatest aid to the beginner in bird study. Among the most useful are the Reed's, "Bird Guides," one covering the birds of the eastern and the other those of the western part of the United States. The pictures alone will be of great use in learning the names of feathered neighbours, while an intelligent study of the text will reveal the identity of many others.

Local lists of such birds as are found in a neighbourhood, or a county, are always a great aid in determining, with a fair degree of accuracy, just what species may or may not be expected to appear in a given locality. Such lists are usually first published in The Auk, The Condor, or other ornithological publications, and in many cases are printed and distributed later as separate pamphlets.

There have been published also many State lists of birds, usually accompanied by detailed information regarding abundance and distribution of all the species known to occur in the State. Every bird {15} student should, if possible, get a copy of his own State bird book. Any reader who may wish to learn if such a list of the birds of his neighbourhood or State has been published is at liberty to address the question to the author of this book.

Movements of Birds.--One does not get very far in the work of bird study without discovering that certain movements are characteristic of various families; and when the observer is able to recognize this difference in manner a long step has been taken in acquiring the power of identifying species.

After watching for a time the actions of a Downy Woodpecker as it clings to the side of a tree, or hops along its bark, one is quick to recognize the Woodpecker manner when some other species of that family is encountered. Recalling the ceaseless activities of a Yellow Warbler the observer feels, without quite knowing why, that he has discovered another Warbler of some kind when a Redstart or Chestnut-sided Warbler appears. Once identify a Barn Swallow coursing through the air, and a long {16} stride is made toward the identification of the Cliff or Tree Swallow when one swings into view. The flight of the Flicker, the Goldfinch, the Nighthawk, and the Sparrow Hawk, is so characteristic in each case that I have often been able to name the bird for a student upon being told its approximate size and the character of its flight. Who can see a Wild Duck swimming, or a Gull flying, without at once referring it to the group of birds to which it belongs? Thus the first step is taken toward learning the names of the species, and the grouping of them into families.

Artificial Cover in Hiding.--When studying the larger or the shyer species it is sometimes well to hide one's self from view with whatever articles are at hand that resemble the natural surroundings. This may be done by covering with hay if in a field, or by holding some leafy branches about you if in the woods.

On a lonely island in Pamlico Sound I once got some fishermen to cover me with sand and sea-shells, and in that way managed to get a close view of {17} the large flocks of Cormorants that came there to roost every night. The island was small and perfectly barren, and any other method of attempted concealment would have failed utterly.

Another time, while crouched among some boulders watching for a flock of Gambel's Quails to come to a water-hole in the Santa Catalina Mountains of Arizona, a Canyon Wren alighted on my back, for I was covered with an old tent fly so spotted with mildew that it closely resembled the neighbouring rocks. A moment later it flew to a point scarcely more than a foot from my face, when, after one terrified look, it departed.

The Umbrella Blind.--A device now often used by ornithologists is the umbrella blind, which is easy to construct. Take a stout umbrella, remove the handle, and insert the end in a hollow brass rod five feet long. Sharpen the rod at the other end and thrust it into the ground. Over the raised umbrella throw a dark green cloth cut and sewed so as to make a curtain that will reach the ground all round. A {19} draw-string will make it fit over the top. Get inside, cut a few vertical observation slits six inches long, and your work is done. Erect this within ten feet of a nest, and leave it alone for a few hours. The birds will quickly get accustomed to it so that later you may go inside and watch at close range without disturbing them in the least. This blind is often used for close bird photography. I have taken pictures of Herring Gulls at a distance of only six feet with the aid of such a blind. If you wish to use it on a windy day it may be stayed by a few guy-lines from the top and sides.

The foregoing instructions include all the necessary aids to a beginner in bird study who desires to start afield properly equipped. To summarize them, all that is really necessary is a field glass, a notebook for memoranda, inconspicuous clothing, and a desire to listen and learn.

In the next chapter we shall discuss some of the things to be learned in the study of the life about the nest.

{20}

NOTE.--The following publications will be found of great aid to the student in identifying wild birds:

"Handbook of Birds of Eastern North America," by Frank M. Chapman, published by D. Appleton Or Company, price $3.65, postpaid.

"Handbook of Birds of Western United States," by Florence Merriam Bailey, published by Houghton, Mifflin Company, price $3.68, postpaid.

"Water and Game Birds: Birds of Prey" and "Land Birds East of the Rockies: From Parrots to Blue Birds," by Chester A. Reed, published by Doubleday, Page & Company, price of each in sock cloth, $1.10, postpaid; inflexible leather, $1.35, postpaid.

Educational Leaflets, published by the National Association of Audubon Societies, New York City, a series of nearly one hundred, price 2 cents each.

CHAPTER II

THE LIFE ABOUT THE NEST

In view of the fact that birds display much activity about their nests there is a great advantage in studying the nesting bird. Once locate an occupied nest, and by quietly watching for a time, your field glass and bird guide will usually enable you to learn the owner's name. If you do not know where any nest is to be found go out and hunt for one. This in itself will be an exciting sport, although it should be pursued with good judgment. Children unattended should not be permitted to hunt nests in spring. A very excellent way to find one is to keep a sharp watch upon birds at the time when they are engaged in nest building.

Nest Hunting.--By noticing every bird suspected of being interested in domestic affairs, you are pretty {22} sure to see one before long with grass, twigs, rootlets, or something of the kind in its bill. Now watch closely, for you are in a fair way to discover a nest. The bird may not go directly to the spot. If it suspects it is being watched it may hop from twig to twig and from bush to bush for many minutes before revealing its secret, and if it becomes very apprehensive it may even drop its burden and begin a search for insects with the air of one who had never even dreamed of building a nest. Even when unsuspicious it will not always go directly to the nest. From an outhouse I once watched a Blue Jay, with a twig, change its perch more than thirty times before going to the fork where its nest was being built.

Sometimes a bird may be induced to reveal its secret by placing in its sight tempting nesting material. By this means Mrs. Pearson last summer found a Redstart's nest. Discovering a female industriously hopping about near the camp, and suspecting what it was seeking, she dropped some ravellings of a white cotton string from the veranda railing, letting {23} them fall where the bird could see them. These proved most acceptable, and the Redstart immediately appropriated them, one at a time, with the result that she soon betrayed her nest.

Early morning is the best time of the day to find birds working at their nests, for then they are most active. Perhaps a reason for this is that the broken twigs, leaves, and dead grasses, wet with the dews of night, are more pliable, and consequently more easily woven into place.

For nesting sites birds as a rule prefer the open country. Rolling meadowlands, with orchards, thickets, and occasional streams, are ideal places for birds in spring.

Number and Colour of Eggs.--The full complement of eggs laid by a bird is known as a set or clutch. The number varies greatly with different species. The Leach's Petrel, Murre, and some other sea birds, have but one egg. The Turkey Vulture, Mourning Dove, Hummingbird, Whip-poor-will, and Nighthawk lay two. Various Thrushes, such as the {24} Robin, Veery, and Wood Thrush, deposit from three to five, four being the most usual number. Wild Ducks, Turkeys, and Grouse range from eight to a dozen or more; while Quails sometimes lay as many as eighteen.

Eggs are variously coloured, and some are so marked that the blending of their colours with those of their surroundings renders them inconspicuous. Thus those of the Killdeer, Sandpiper, and Nighthawk, for example, are not easily distinguished from the ground on which they lie.

Many eggs that are laid in holes or other dark places are white without markings of any kind, as illustrated by those of the Chimney Swift, Belted Kingfisher, and all Woodpeckers. In such instances Nature shows no disposition to be lavish with her colouring matter where it is not needed.

Behaviour When Nest Is Discovered.--After the young are hatched it is even easier to find nests by watching the parents. The nestlings are hungry at all hours, and the old ones are visiting the nest at frequent intervals throughout the day. Birds {25} behave very differently when their nests are discovered. A Cuckoo will glide away instantly and will make no effort to dispute your possession of her treasures. A Crow will also fly off, and so will a Wild Duck and some others. On the other hand, the Mockingbird, Robin, or Shrike, will raise a great outcry and bring about her half the birds of the neighbourhood to pour out on you their vials of wrath, unless you have the good judgment to retire at once to a respectful distance. Warblers will flit from bush to bush uttering cries of distress and showing their uneasiness. The Mourning Dove, Nighthawk, and many others will feign lameness and seek to lead you away in a vain pursuit. A still larger number will employ the same means of deception after the young have been hatched, as, for example, the Quail, Killdeer, Sandpiper, and Grouse.

However much a bird may resent your intrusion on the privacy of its sanctuary, it is very rare for one to attack you. I remember, however, a boy who once had the bad manners to put his hand into a {26} Cardinal's nest and had a finger well bitten for his misdeed. Beware, too, of trying to caress a Screech Owl sitting on its eggs in a hollow tree; its claws are very sharp, and you will need first-aid attention if you persist. Occasionally some bird will let you stroke its back before deserting its eggs, and may even let you take its photograph while you are thus engaged. On one occasion I removed a Turkey Vulture's egg from beneath the sitting bird. It merely hissed feebly as I approached, and a moment later humbly laid at my feet a portion of the carrion which it had eaten a short time before--a well-meant but not wholly appreciated peace-offering.

Lessons to Be Learned.--An infinite variety of interesting things may be learned by watching birds at their nests, or by a study of the nests themselves. How many persons have ever tried to answer seriously the old conundrum: "How many straws go to make a bird's nest?" Let us examine critically one nest and see what we find. One spring after a red squirrel had destroyed the three eggs in a Veery's {27} nest which I had had under observation, I determined to study carefully its composition, knowing the birds would not want to make use of it again. The nest rested among the top limbs of a little brush-pile and was just two feet above the ground. Some young shoots had grown up through the brush and their leaves partly covered the nest from view. It had an extreme breadth of ten inches and was five inches high. The inner cup was two and one-half inches deep, and measured the same across the top. In its construction two small weed stalks and eleven slender twigs were used. The latter were from four and one-half to eight inches long. The main bulk of the nest was made up of sixty-eight large leaves, besides a mass of decayed leaf fragments. Inside this bed was the inner nest, composed of strips of soft bark. Assembling this latter material I found that when compressed with the hands its bulk was about the size of a baseball. Among the decaying leaves near the base of the nest three beetles and a small snail had found a home.

The Veery, in common with a large number of other birds, builds a nest open at the top. The eggs, therefore, are often more or less exposed to the Crow, the pilfering Jay, and the egg-stealing red squirrel. This necessitates a very close and careful watch on the part of the owners. At times it may seem that the birds are not in sight, and that the eggs are deserted; but let the observer go too near, and invariably one or both old birds will let him know of their presence by voicing their resentment and sending abroad their cries of distress.

Character of Material Used.--A wide variety of material is used by birds that build open nests. Cotton and feathers enter largely into the composition of the lining of a Shrike's nest. In Florida the Mockingbird shows a decided preference for the withered leaves and stems of life-everlasting, better known as the plant that produces "rabbit tobacco." The nest of the Summer Tanager is made almost entirely of grasses, the outer half being green, freshly plucked blades that contrast strikingly with the {29} brown inner layer with which the nest is lined. Many of the Thrushes make use of large flat leaves, and also of rags and pieces of paper. Robins stiffen their nests by making in them a substantial cup of mud, which, when dry, adds greatly to the solidity of the structure. On the island of Cape Hatteras there are many sheep, and many Prairie Warblers of the region make their nests entirely of wool.

The most dainty structure built, in this country, by the bill and feet of birds, is the nest made by the Ruby-throated Hummingbird. When completed it is scarcely larger than an English walnut, and is saddled on a small horizontal limb of a tree, often many feet from the ground. It is composed almost entirely of soft plant fibres, fragments of spiders' webs sometimes being used to hold them in shape. The outer sides are thickly studded with bits of lichen, and practised, indeed, is the eye of the man or woman that can distinguish it from a knot on a limb. Although the Hummingbird's nest is exceedingly frail, there is nothing on record to show that {30} any great number of them come to grief during the summer rains. It is, however, not called upon for a long term of occupation. Within a month after the two white eggs are laid the young depart on their tiny pinions. Young birds that require a longer period for growth before leaving the nest are furnished usually with more enduring abiding places. {31} In the case of the Bald Eagle, the young of which do not fly until they are many weeks old, a most substantial structure is provided.

It was on the twentieth of January, a number of years ago, that the writer was first delighted by the sight of a Bald Eagle's nest. It was in an enormous pine tree growing in a swamp in central Florida, and being ambitious to examine its contents, I determined to climb to the great eyrie in the topmost crotch of the tree, one hundred and thirty-one feet above the earth. By means of climbing-irons and a rope that passed around the tree and around my body, I slowly ascended, nailing cleats for support as I advanced. After two hours of toil the nest was reached, but another twenty minutes were required to tear aside enough of the structure to permit climbing up one of the limbs on which it rested. In doing this there were brought to view several layers of decayed twigs, pine straw, and fish bones, showing that the birds had been using the nest for many years. Season after season the huge structure had been enlarged by {33} additions until now it was nearly five feet in thickness and about four feet across the top.

At this date it contained two fledglings perhaps three weeks old. Having been led to believe that Eagles were ferocious birds when their nests were approached, it was with feelings of relief that I noticed the parents flying about at long rifle-range. The female, which, as is usual with birds of prey, was the larger of the pair, once or twice swept within twenty yards of my head, but quickly veered off and resumed her former action of beating back and forth over the tree-tops two hundred yards away.

Nests in Holes.--The members of the Woodpecker family, contrary to certain popular beliefs, do not lay their eggs in hollow trees but deposit them in cavities that they excavate for the purpose. The bird student will soon learn just where to look for the nest of each species. Thus you may find the nesting cavity of the Red-headed Woodpecker in a tall stump or dead tree; in some States it is a common bird in towns, and often digs its cavity in a telephone {34} pole. Some years ago a pair excavated a nest and reared their young in a wooden ball on the staff of the dome of the State House in Raleigh, North Carolina.

On the plains, where trees are few, the telegraph poles provide convenient nesting sites for Woodpeckers of various species. While travelling on a slow train through Texas I counted one hundred and fifty telegraph poles in succession, thirty-nine of which contained Woodpeckers' holes. Probably I did not see all of them, for not over two-thirds of the surface of each pole was visible from the car window. Not all of these holes, of course, were occupied by Woodpeckers in any one season.

Flickers, or "Yellowhammers," use dead trees as a rule, but sometimes make use of a living tree by digging the nest out of the dead wood where a knot hole offers a convenient opening. The only place I have ever known them regularly to nest in living trees is in the deserts of Arizona, where the saguaro or "tree cactus" is about the only tree large enough to be employed for such a purpose. In the {35} Northern States Flickers sometimes chisel holes through the weatherboarding of ice-houses and make cavities for their eggs in the tightly packed sawdust within. They have been known also to lay their eggs in nesting boxes put up for their accommodation.

In travelling through the pine barrens of the Southern States one frequently finds grouped about the negroes' cabins and plantation houses the popular chinaberry, or Pride of India tree. Here are the places to look for the nest of the Hairy Woodpecker. In that country, in fact, I have never found a nest of this bird except in the dead, slanting limb of a chinaberry tree.

The member of this family which displays most originality in its nest building is the Red-cockaded Woodpecker. It is a Southern bird, and the abode for its young is always chiselled from a living pitch-pine tree. This, in itself, is very unusual for any of our eastern Woodpeckers. The bird, however, has a still stranger habit. For two or three feet above the {36} entrance hole, and for five or six feet below it, all around the tree, innumerable small openings are dug through to the inner bark. From these little wells pour streams of soft resin that completely cover the bark and give the trunk a white, glistening appearance, which is visible sometimes for a quarter of a mile. Just why they do this has never been explained. It is true, however, that the sticky resin prevents ants and flying squirrels from reaching the nest, and both of these are known to be troublesome to eggs and young birds.

A simple plan, which is usually successful in finding out if a Woodpecker is at home in its nesting hole, is to strike a few sharp blows on the tree with some convenient club or rock. After a little treatment of this kind the bird will often come to the entrance and look down, as if to inquire into the meaning of all the disturbance. If the nest has been newly made many fragments of small chips of wood will be found on the ground beneath the tree.

Variety of Situations.--The student who takes up {37} the subject of nest architecture will soon be impressed not only with the wide assortment of materials used, but also with the wonderful variety of situations chosen.

The Grebe, or "Water Witch," builds one of the most remarkable nests of any American bird. It is a floating raft, the buoyant part of which is the green {38} stems of water plants, not bent over, but severed from their roots and piled across one another. On this platform is collected decaying vegetation gathered from beneath the water. Here the eggs are deposited, and are carefully covered with more decaying vegetation when the bird desires to be absent from the nest.

Variation in Families.--Sometimes there is wide variety in the character of the nests of different species classified as belonging to the same family. The Flycatcher group is a good example of this fact. Here we have as one member of the family the Kingbird, that makes a heavy bulky nest often on one of the upper, outermost limbs of an apple tree. The Wood Pewee's nest is a frail, shallow excuse for a nest, resting securely on a horizontal limb of some well-grown tree. Then there is the Phoebe, that plasters its cup-shaped mass of nesting material with mud, thus securing it to a rafter or other projection beneath a bridge, outbuilding, or porch roof. Still farther away from the typical Flycatcher's {39} nest is that made by a perfectly regular member of the family, the Great-crested Flycatcher. The straw and other substances it collects as a bed for its eggs and young is carried into some hollow tree, old Woodpecker hole, or nesting box. Often a cast-off skin of a snake is used, and sometimes the end is permitted to hang out of the hole--a sort of "scare-crow," perhaps, intended for the notice of annoying neighbours.

Meagre Nests.--Heretofore, mention has been made only of the nests of birds built with much labour and usually constructed in trees or bushes. A very large number of species, however, lay their eggs on the ground with little or no attempt to gather around or beneath them any special nesting material. The Killdeer's eggs are simply deposited in a slight hole scratched in the earth, usually in an open field or on a rocky hillside. The only lining is a few grass blades or smooth pebbles. To protect them from enemies the birds depend much upon the peculiar marking of the eggs, which makes them look like the {40} ground on which they lie, and this seems to be a sufficient safeguard for the eggs and offspring of the species. The Nighthawk lays her two eggs on the bare ground in a field or open woods; and the Whip-poor-will's nest is on the fallen leaves of a thicket at any spot which the bird happens to select.

The Gulls so common along our coast and about the larger lakes make substantial nests, as a rule--but not always. I have found them on the islands along the coast of Maine containing not a dozen blades of grass, a seemingly scant protection against the danger of rolling away to destruction.

On the sandy islands of the Atlantic Coast, from Long Island southward, many species of Terns make nests by simply burrowing a slight depression in the sand among the sea-shells. Some of the sea birds of the far North, as, for example, the Murres and Auks, often lay their eggs on the shelving cliffs exposed to the sweep of the ocean gales. These are shaped as if designed by nature to prevent them rolling off the rocks. They are very large at one {41} end and toward the other taper sharply. When the wind blows they simply swing around in circles.

Although we sometimes speak of the bird's nest as its home, such really is not the case, for the nest of the wild bird is simply the cradle for the young. When the little ones have flown it is seldom that either they or their parents ever return to its shelter.

CHAPTER III

DOMESTIC LIFE OF THE BIRDS

It is a privilege to be so situated that one may watch from day to day the occurrences about a wild bird's nest. Here feathered life reaches its greatest heights of emotion, and comedies and threatened tragedies are of daily occurrence. The people we know best are those whom we have seen at their play and at their work, in moments of elation and doubt, and in times of great happiness and dire distress. And so it is that he who has followed the activities of a pair of birds through all the joys and anxieties of nest building, brooding, and of caring for the young, may well lay claim to a close acquaintanceship with them.

In watching a nest one will learn, for example, that with most of our small birds both parents engage in {43} the pleasant duty of feeding the young, at times shielding the little ones from the hot rays of the sun with their half-extended wings, and now and then driving away intruders. The common passerine birds also attend carefully to the sanitation of the nest and remove the feces, which is inclosed in a membrane and is thus easily carried in the bill. This is usually dropped several yards away. If allowed to accumulate on the ground beneath the nest it might attract the attention of some prowling enemy and lead to a disastrous discovery.

Parental Care of Young.--There is a wide difference in the relative helplessness of nesting birds, and a corresponding difference in the methods of parental care. The young of praecocial birds are able to run or swim with their parents almost as soon as hatched, for they not only have the strength to do this, but their bodies being covered with down they are protected from the sun or cold. Examples of such birds are the Quail, Grouse, Sandpipers, Plovers, and Ducks. The young of these and allied species are {44} able from the beginning to pick up their food, and they quickly learn from the example of their parents what is desirable. Soon they are able to shift for themselves, although one or both of the parents continue to attend them until grown.

With the altricial birds the young are hatched in an absolutely helpless condition, being both blind and naked, and it is necessary that they be fed by the parents, not only while occupying the nest, but also for several weeks afterward. To this group belong most of the small birds we are accustomed to see about the house. When newly born the food they receive is first digested in the crop or the stomach of the parent from which it is regurgitated into the mouth of the young. Flickers, Hummingbirds, Doves, and some others continue to feed their young in this manner, but usually the method soon gives way to that, more commonly observed, of simply supplying soft-bodied insects which have been captured and killed but not eaten.

In the case of Pelicans, Cormorants, and Ibises, {45} the young thrust their bills far down the throats of the parents to procure the regurgitated food.

From this custom the ancients may have got the idea that Pelicans feed their young with their own life blood. The suggestion still persists, and on the seal of one of our large life insurance companies of America a Pelican and her young are represented accompanied with the motto: "I live and die for those I love." The great seal of the State of Louisiana uses a similar picture without the motto.

Hawks and Owls tear their prey to pieces and on this the young feed at infrequent intervals. Sometimes several hours pass between the visits of the food-laden parents, but the supply is usually adequate when at length it arrives.

Sharing the Labours.--Most young birds, however, are fed with great frequency. For more than an hour one day the writer watched a pair of Georgia Mockingbirds feeding their young. The one that appeared to be the female visited the nest with food on an average once every two minutes, and the male {46} made a similar trip about once in twelve minutes. He could have done better had he not spent so much time flying aimlessly about and scolding imaginary enemies.

Some birds have what seem to be very curious habits at the nesting time. The jealous-hearted Hornbill of the Old World never trusts his spouse to wander away from the nest after her duties there once begin. In order that he may always know just where she is he quite willingly undertakes to supply her with all her food during the days while the incubation of the eggs is going forward. With mud he daubs up the entrance to the hollow in the tree where she is sitting, leaving only a small opening through which food may be passed. When the mud has dried it becomes very hard and the patient mate is an absolute prisoner until the day comes when she passes the word to her lord that the eggs have hatched, and he sets her free.

In our own western country there dwells a bird known as the Phalarope, the females of which enjoy {47} an immunity from domestic duties that might cause the lady Hornbill many an envious sigh did she know of the freedom of her American sister.

Mrs. Phalarope has no intention of being shut in with her eggs for a month while her mate goes roaming at large about the country, nor has she any idea of playing the part of the Georgia Mockingbird and bringing five-sixths of the food which the young require. Her method of procedure is first to permit her mate to search for a suitable nesting site. When some sheltered spot in the ground, quite to her liking, has been found she deposits the eggs and goes her way. Little companies of female Phalaropes may be seen at this time of the year frequenting the ponds and sloughs they inhabit. The dutiful and well-trained males are all at home, where they are responsible for the entire task of caring for, and incubating, the eggs.

Length of Mated Life.--The length of time which birds remain mated is a question often asked but seldom answered satisfactorily. The truth of the {48} matter is that not much is known about the subject. Apparently a great many birds return to the same yard and even to the same tree to build their nest year after year. I say apparently because such birds are seldom marked in such a way as to enable one to be positive that they are the identical individuals which came the year before. It is probably somewhere near the truth to say that most small birds usually choose the same mates year after year if both survive the dangers of winter and in spring meet again on their old trysting grounds. It is safe to assert that as a rule birds retain the same mates throughout the breeding season if misfortune does not befall one of them. During the fall and winter months, when the impulses governing domestic duties are dormant, birds pay little or no attention to their mates.

A Much-married Bluebird.--One spring a pair of Bluebirds came into our yard, and to the accompaniment of much cheerful bird conversation, in the form of whistles, twitters, chirps, and snatches of {49} song, began hunting eagerly for some place to locate a nest. Out in the woodshed I found a box, perhaps six inches square and twice as long. Cutting a small entrance hole on one side, I fastened the box seven or eight feet from the ground on the side of a young tree. The newcomers immediately took possession and began carrying dry grasses into their adopted sanctuary. Several days elapsed and then one morning, while standing on the back of a garden settee and peeping into the hole, I discovered that a pale-blue egg had been laid. When the nest contained four of these little beauties incubation began.

One rainy night while the mother bird was on duty she must have heard the scratching of claws on the box outside. A moment later two yellow eyes blazed at the entrance and a long arm reached into the nest. The next morning on the grass beneath the window we found her wing tips and many other fragments of her plumage. All that day the distressed mate flew about the lawn and called continually. He seemed to gather but little food and {50} the evidence of his suffering was pitiful. In fact, he stirred our feelings to such a pitch we at length closed the windows to shut out the sounds of his mournful calls.

Upon looking out next morning, the first note we heard was that of a Bluebird, but his voice seemed to have lost some of its sorrow. Walking around the corner of the house, I found him sitting on a limb near the box. Two feet from him sat another Bluebird--a female. At eleven o'clock we saw her clinging to the side of the box and looking inquiringly into the entrance hole. We knew what this meant; incidentally we knew, too, that being a ladybird she would have no use for the nest and eggs that had been placed there by another, so I cleaned out the box.

We were anxious that the cat should have no chance to destroy our little friend's second wife, so the box was suspended from a limb by a wire over two feet in length. Five eggs were laid and the mother bird began sitting. Then one night the cat {51} found out what was happening. How she ever succeeded in her undertaking, I know not. She must have started by climbing the tree and creeping out on the limb. I have never seen a cat slide down a wire; nevertheless the next morning the box was tenantless and the feathers of the second female were scattered over the lawn. This time the Bluebird's heart seemed really broken and his cries of lamentation filled the grove. Eleven days now passed before a third soul-mate came to share his fortunes. We could afford to take no more risks. On a sunny hillside in the garden the cat was buried, and a few weeks later four little Bluebirds left the lawn on their own wings.

The Faithful Canada Geese.--Along the Atlantic Coast, where the shooting of wildfowl is an important industry with many people, the raising of Canada Geese is a common custom. Not only do these great birds serve as food, but they play the part of decoys when their owners go ahunting. They are genuine Wild Geese, some of them having been {52} wounded and captured from the great flocks which frequent these waters during the colder months of the year. They retain their wild characteristics with great tenacity and it is necessary to keep them pinioned to prevent their flying away to the North when in spring the spirit of migration calls aloud to all the bird world.

The conduct of these decoys indicates that the losing of a mate is a much more serious matter among them than with the Bluebird and others of our small feathered friends. When a gander has chosen his goose and she has accepted his advances, the pair remain constantly together, summer and winter, as long as they live. If one is killed, many years may elapse before the survivor selects another companion.

In Currituck County, North Carolina, there was not long ago a gander that local tradition said was sixty-two years of age. The first thirty years of his life he remained unmated and for the last thirty-two he has been the proud possessor of a mate from whose side he has never strayed.

These Geese do not mate readily, and a man who has a company of thirty or forty may well be satisfied if six or eight pairs of them are mated. The truth of this statement is proved by the fact that on the local market a single Goose is worth about one dollar, while a pair of mated Geese will readily bring five dollars.

Unmated Birds.--A little reflection will make the student realize the fact that out in the fields and woods, in the swamps and on the mountains, on the beaches, as well as far away on the ocean, there are many birds that are not mated. Among them are widows and widowers, heartfree spinsters and pining bachelors. Just what per cent. of the bird life is unmated in any one season it would, of course, be impossible to tell. The information which the writer has gathered by a careful census of a certain species in a given limited territory enabled him to determine that in this particular case only about three-fifths of the individuals are mated any one season.

Polygamy Among Birds.--As with mankind, some races have well-developed tendencies toward polygamy. In the warmer regions of the United States there dwells a great, splendid, glossy Blackbird, the Boat-tailed Crackle. The nest of this bird is a wonderfully woven structure of water plants and grasses and is usually built in a bush growing in the {55} water. When you find one nest of the Crackle you are pretty certain to find several other occupied nests in the immediate vicinity. From three to six of these marvellous cradles, with their quiet brown female owners, often appear to be watched over by one shining, iridescent lord Crackle, who may be husband to them all. He guards his own with jealous care. Evidently, too, he desires the whole country to know that he is the most handsome, ferocious bird on the earth; for all day long his hoarse shoutings may be heard, and when he launches into the air, the sound of the ponderous beating of his wings can, on a still day, be heard half a mile away, across the lake.

One of the best-known polygamous birds of North America is the Wild Turkey. Go into any part of the country where this fast-disappearing game bird still survives, and the experienced local gunners will tell you that in the mating season you will usually find a gobbler accompanied by two or more Turkey hens. When a female gets ready to make her nest she slips away from her sultan and the other members {56} of the seraglio and, going to some broom-sedge field or open place in the woods, constructs her nest on the ground beneath some slight, convenient shelter. Day after day she absents herself for a short time, and the speckled treasures grow in number until from twelve to fifteen have been deposited. All this time her movements are characterized by absolute secrecy, for if the gobbler by any chance comes upon the nest he immediately breaks every egg. He is perhaps wise enough to know that when his hens begin to set lonely times are in store for him.

The Outcast.--One of our wild birds whose domestic relations are not fully understood is strongly suspected of being promiscuously polygamous. Suspicion on this point is heightened by the fact that it never has a nest even of the most humble character, and shuns absolutely all the ordinary dangers and responsibilities of parentage. We call this seemingly unnatural creature the Cowbird, probably because it is often seen feeding in pastures {57} among cattle, where it captures many insects disturbed into activity by the movements of the browsing animals.

The Cowbird lays its eggs in the nests of various other birds, distributing them about the neighbourhood. Here they are left to be hatched and the young to be reared by the foster parents. Cowbird's eggs have been found in the nests of nearly one hundred species of birds, and nearly always the nest of some smaller bird is chosen. Despite this fact the Cowbird's eggs are often first to hatch. The young grow rapidly and, being strong and aggressive, not only secure the lion's share of the food, but frequently crowd the young of the rightful owner out of the nest to perish on the ground beneath.

As soon as the young leave the nest the greedy Cowbird follows the little mother about the thickets, shouting loudly for food. Its fierce clamour drowns the weaker cries of the legitimate young, which I have reason to believe even then often die for lack {58} of nourishment. So insistent is the young Cowbird and so persistently does it pursue the foster parent that it is well cared for and invariably thrives. It is no uncommon sight, during the days of June and July, to see a worn, bedraggled Song Sparrow {59} working desperately in a frantic effort to feed one or more great hulking Cowbirds twice its size. It is little wonder that discerning people are not fond of the Cowbird. Even the birds seem to regard it as an outcast from avian society, and rarely associate with it on friendly terms. This is the only species of North American birds that exhibits such depravity.

All other birds display great willingness to attend to their home duties, and often give evidence of keen delight while so engaged. One of the most exquisite and dainty forms of bird life found in the United States is the little Blue-gray Gnatcatcher. When occupied in building the nest, which is usually saddled on the limb of some forest tree, the birds call to each other constantly; and even after the eggs are laid there is no attempt to restrain their expressions of happiness. Unlike the Crow and Jay, that sometimes appropriate the nests of other birds, these little creatures have no sins to answer for to their neighbours. One of the most pleasing sights I {60} have witnessed was a male Gnatcatcher that had relieved his mate at the nest. He was sitting on the eggs and, with head thrown back, sang with all his might, apparently unconscious of the evil which such gaiety might bring upon his household.

CHAPTER IV

THE MIGRATION OF BIRDS

There is something fascinating about the word migration. It sends our minds back to the dim stories of tribal movements carved on the rocks by men who wrought in the dawn of history. We wonder at the compelling force that drove our ancestors through the forests of northern Germany, or caused the Aztecs to cross the Mexican deserts. It calls to something in our blood, for even the most stolid must at times hearken to the Pied Piper and with Kipling feel that "On the other side the world we're overdue."

Man is not alone the possessor of the migrating passion. Menhaden, in vast schools, sweep along our Atlantic Coast in their season. From unknown regions of the ocean herring and salmon return to {62} the streams of their nativity when the spirit of migration sweeps over the shoals into the abysmal depths. There are butterflies that in companies rise from mud puddles beside the road and go dancing away to the South in autumn. The caribou, in long streams, come southward over the barrens of Labrador when the word is passed, and even squirrels, over extended regions, have been known to migrate en masse for hundreds of miles. There is, however, no phase of the life of birds which is quite so distinctive. The extent and duration of their migrations are among the most wonderful phenomena of the natural world.

Ornithologists have gathered much information regarding their coming and going, but knowledge on many of the points involved is incomplete. It is only of recent years that the nest of the Solitary Sandpiper has been found, and yet this is a very common bird in the eastern United States in certain seasons. Where is the scientist who can yet tell us in what country the common Chimney Swift {63} passes the winter, or over what stretches of sea and land the Arctic Tern passes when journeying between its summer home in the Arctic seas and its winter abode in the Antarctic wastes? The main fact, however, that the great majority of birds of the Northern Hemisphere go south in autumn and return in spring, is well known.

Moulting.--By the time the young are able to care for themselves the plumage of the hard-working parents is worn and frayed and a new suit of feathers becomes necessary. They do not acquire this all at once. The feathers drop out gradually from the various feather tracts over the body, and their places are at once taken by a new growth. While this is going on the birds are less in evidence than at other times. They keep out of sight and few song notes are heard. Perhaps there is some irritation and unpleasantness connected with moulting which causes a dejection of spirit.

With swimming water birds the wing quills disappear nearly all at once and the birds are unable {64} for a short time to fly; but being at home in the water, where they secure their food, they are not left in the helpless, even desperate, condition in which a land bird would find itself if unable to fly. In a few cases birds begin to migrate before this moulting takes place, but with the great majority the moult is complete before they leave their summer homes.

Why Birds Migrate.--Why birds migrate we can only conjecture. Without doubt the growing scarcity of food in autumn is the controlling factor with many of them; and this would seem to be an excellent reason for leaving the region of their summer sojourn. Cold weather alone would not drive all of them southward, else why do many small birds pass the winter in northern latitudes where severe climatic conditions prevail? Should we assume the failing food supply to be the sole cause of migration, we would find ourselves at fault when we came to consider that birds leave the tropic regions in spring, when food is still exceedingly abundant, and journey northward thousands of miles to their former summer haunts.

There is a theory held by many naturalists that the migrating instinct dates back to the glacial period. According to this theory North America was inhabited originally by non-migrating birds. Then the great Arctic ice-cap began to move southward and the birds were forced to flee before it or starve. Now and then during the subsequent period the ice receded and the birds returned, only to be driven again before the next onrush of the Ice King. Thus during these centuries of alternate advance and retreat of the continental glacier, the birds acquired a habit, which later became an instinct, of retreating southward upon the approach of cold weather and coming back again when the ice and snow showed indications of passing away.

The Gathering Flocks.--To the bird student there is keen delight in watching for the first spring arrivals and noting their departure with the dying year. It is usually in August that we first observe an unwonted restlessness on the part of our birds which tells us that they have begun to hear the call of the {66} South. The Blackbirds assemble in flocks and drift aimlessly about the fields. Every evening for weeks they will collect a chattering multitude in the trees of some lawn, or in those skirting a village street, and there at times cause great annoyance to their human neighbours.

Across the Hudson River from New York, in the Hackensack marshes, behind the Palisades, clouds of Swallows collect in the late summer evenings, and for many days one may see them from the car windows as they glide through the upper air or swarm to roost among the rushes. These Swallows and the Blackbirds are getting together before starting on their fall migration.

In Greensboro, North Carolina, there is a small grove of trees clustered about the courthouse which is a very busy place during the nights of summer. Here, before the first of July, Purple Martins begin to collect of an evening. In companies of hundreds and thousands, they whirl about over the tops of the houses, alight in the trees, and then almost {67} immediately dash upward and away again. Not till dark do they finally settle to roost. Until late at night a great chorus of voices may be heard among the branches. The multitude increases daily for six or eight weeks, additions, in the form of new family groups, constantly augmenting their numbers. Some time in September the migration call reaches the Martins, and, yielding to its spell, they at once depart toward their winter home in tropical South America.

The Usual Movement.--Many of our smaller birds, such as Warblers and Vireos, do not possess a strong flocking instinct, but, nevertheless, they may be seen associated in numbers during the season of the northern and southern movements. Such birds migrate chiefly at night and have been observed through telescopes at high altitudes. Such observations are made by pointing the telescope at the disk of the full moon on clear nights. On cloudy or foggy nights the birds fly lower, as may be known by the clearer sounds of their calls as they pass over; at times one may even hear the flutter of their wings. There is a {68} good reason for their travelling at this time, as they need the daylight for gathering food.

There appear to be certain popular pathways of migration along which many, though by no means all, of the aerial voyageurs wing their way. As to the distribution of these avian highways, we know at least that the coastlines of the continents are favourite routes. Longfellow, in the valley of the Charles, lived beneath one of these arteries of migration, and on still autumn nights often listened to the voices of the migrating hosts, "falling dreamily through the sky."

A small number of the species migrate by day; among these are the Hawks, Swallows, Ducks, and Geese. The last two groups also travel by night. The rate at which they proceed on their journey is not as great as was formerly supposed. From twenty to thirty miles an hour is the speed generally taken, and perhaps fifty miles an hour is the greatest rapidity attained. Flights are usually not long sustained, a hundred and fifty miles a day being above the {69} average. Individuals will at times pause and remain for a few days in a favourable locality before proceeding farther. When large bodies of water are encountered longer flights are of course necessary, for land birds cannot rest on the water as their feathers would soon become water-soaked and drowning would result. Multitudes of small birds, including even the little Ruby-throated Hummingbird, annually cross the Gulf of Mexico at a single flight. This necessitates a continuous journey of from five hundred to seven hundred miles. Some North American birds migrate southward only a few hundred miles to pass the winter, while many others go from Canada and the United States to Mexico, Central and South America.

The ponds and sloughs of all that vast country lying between the Great Lakes and Hudson Bay on the east and the mountains of the Far West, constitute the principal nursery of North American waterfowl, whence, in autumn, come the flocks of Ducks and Geese that in winter darken the Southern {70} sounds and lakes. One stream moves down the Pacific Coast, another follows the Mississippi Valley to the marshes of Louisiana and Texas, while a third passes diagonally across the country in a southeasterly direction until it reaches the Maryland and Virginia coastline. Thence the birds disperse along the coastal country from Maine to Florida.

The Travelling Shore Birds.--Turnstones, Sanderlings, Curlews, and other denizens of the beaches and salt marshes migrate in great numbers along our Atlantic Coast. Some of them winter in the United States, and others pass on to the West Indies and southward. The extent of the annual journeys undertaken by some of these birds is indeed marvellous. Admiral Peary has told me that he found shore birds on the most northern land, where it slopes down into the Arctic Sea, less than five hundred miles from the North Pole; and these same birds pass the winter seven thousand miles south of their summer home. One of these wonderful migrants is the Golden Plover. In autumn the birds leave {72} eastern North America at Nova Scotia, striking out boldly across the Atlantic Ocean, and they may not again sight land until they reach the West Indies or the northern coast of South America. Travelling, as they do, in a straight line, they ordinarily pass eastward of the Bermuda Islands. Upon reaching South America, after a flight of two thousand four hundred miles across the sea, they move on down to Argentina and northern

Patagonia. In spring they return by an entirely different route. Passing up through western South America, and crossing the Gulf of Mexico, these marvellous travellers follow up the Mississippi Valley to their breeding grounds on the shores of the Arctic Ocean. Their main lines of spring and fall migration are separated by as much as two thousand miles. During the course of the year the Golden Plover takes a flight of sixteen thousand miles.

The World's Migrating Champion.--The bird which makes the longest flight, according to the late Wells W. Cooke, America's greatest authority on bird migration, is the Arctic Tern. Professor Cooke, to {73} whom we owe so much of our knowledge of the subject, says of this bird:

"It deserves its title of 'arctic' for it nests as far North as land has been discovered; that is, as far North as the bird can find anything stable on which to construct its nest. Indeed, so arctic are the conditions under which it breeds that the first nest found by man in this region, only seven and one-half degrees from the pole, contained a downy chick surrounded by a wall of newly fallen snow that had been scooped out of the nest by the parent. When the young are full grown the entire family leaves the Arctic, and several months later they are found skirting the edge of the Antarctic continent.

"What their track is over that eleven thousand miles of intervening space no one knows. A few scattered individuals have been noted along the United States coast south to Long Island, but the great flocks of thousands and thousands of these Terns which range from pole to pole have never been noted by ornithologists competent to indicate their {74} preferred route and their time schedule. The Arctic Terns arrive in the Far North about June fifteenth and leave about August twenty-fifth, thus staying fourteen weeks at the nesting site. They probably spend a few weeks longer in the winter than in the summer home, and this would leave them scarcely twenty weeks for the round trip of twenty-two thousand miles. Not less than one hundred and fifty miles in a straight line must be their daily task, and this is undoubtedly multiplied several times by their zigzag twistings and turnings in pursuit of food.

"The Arctic Tern has more hours of daylight and sunlight than any other animal on the globe. At the most northern nesting site the midnight sun has already appeared before the birds' arrival, and it never sets during their entire stay at the breeding grounds. During two months of their sojourn in the Antarctic the birds do not see a sunset, and for the rest of the time the sun dips only a little way below the horizon and broad daylight is continuous. The birds, therefore, have twenty-four hours of daylight for at least {75} eight months in the year, and during the other four months have considerably more daylight than darkness."

Perils of Migration.--The periods of migration are fraught with numerous perils for the travelling hosts. Attracted and blinded by the torches of lighthouses, multitudes of birds are annually killed by striking against lighthouse towers in thick, foggy weather. The keeper of the Cape Hatteras light once showed me a chipped place in the lens which he said had been made by the bill of a great white Gannet which one thick night crashed through the outer protecting glass of the lighthouse lamp. As many as seven hundred birds in one month have killed themselves by flying against the Bartholdi Statue of Liberty in New York Harbour. As its torch is no longer lighted the death-rate here has been greatly reduced, although some birds are still killed by flying against the statue. Many were formerly killed by striking the Washington Monument, the record for one night being one hundred and fifty dead birds.

Locomotive engineers have stated that in foggy weather birds often hurl themselves against the headlight and frequently their bodies are later picked up from the engine platform beneath. Birds seem rarely to lose their sense of direction, and they pursue their way for hundreds of miles across the trackless ocean. Terns, Gulls, and Murres are known to go many miles in quest of food for their young and return through dense fogs with unerring directness to their nests.

During the spring it is not uncommon for strange waterfowl to be found helpless in the streets or fields of a region in which they are ordinarily unknown. These birds have become exhausted during the storm of the night before, or have been injured by striking telephone or telegraph wires, an accident which often happens. Once I picked up a Loon after a stormy night. Apparently it had recovered its strength after a few hours' rest, but, as this bird can rise on the wing only from a body of water, over the surface of which it can paddle and flap for many rods, and as {78} there was no pond or lake in all the neighbouring country, the Loon's fate was evident from the first.

Birds are often swept to sea by storm winds from off shore. Vainly they beat against the gale or fly on quivering wings before its blast, until the hungry waves swallow their weary bodies. One morning in northern Lake Michigan I found a Connecticut Warbler lying dead on the deck beneath my stateroom window after a stormy night of wind and rain. Overtaken many miles from shore, this little waif had been able to reach the steamer on the deck of which it had fallen exhausted and died. What of its companions of the night before?

On May 3, 1915, I was on a ship two hundred miles off Brunswick, Georgia. That day the following birds came aboard, all in an exhausted condition: Brown Creeper, Spotted Sandpiper, Green Heron, and Yellow-billed Cuckoo. We also encountered three flocks of Bobolinks, which for some distance flew beside the ship. They appeared to be lost, for they all left us finally, flying straight ahead of the ship, {79} which was bound South, yet birds were supposed to be going North at this season. I wonder if in their bewilderment they mistook the ship for some immense bird pointing the way to land and safety!

Keeping Migration Records.--More than thirty {80} years ago the United States Government put into operation a plan for collecting and tabulating information concerning the dates on which migratory birds reach various points in their journeys. More than two thousand different observers located in various parts of the country have contributed to these records, many of the observers reporting annually through a long series of years. As a result of this carefully gathered material, with the addition of many data collected from other sources, there is now on file in Washington an immense volume of valuable information, much of which, in condensed printed form, is obtainable by the public. This work was in charge of Professor Wells W. Cooke, Biologist, in the Biological Survey of the United States Department of Agriculture until his lamented death in the spring of 1916. Who will take charge of it hereafter is not yet determined; but students may obtain from the director of the Survey migration schedule blanks upon application, and bulletins describing the emigration habits of various North American birds. {81} Watching for the annual appearance of the first individual of each species is most fascinating occupation.

Note.--Government bulletins on the migration of various North American birds may be obtained free, or at slight cost, by addressing H. W. Henshaw, Chief Biological Survey, Department of Agriculture, Washington, D. C.

CHAPTER V

THE BIRDS IN WINTER

With the approach of winter the country loses its charm for many people. The blossoms and verdure, so common yet so beloved by all, have departed, and only the brown expanses of dead grass and weeds relieve the blackness of the forest trees. Even ardent nature lovers have been known to forsake their walks at this season when the songs of the birds have ceased and the forest boughs give forth only sobs and shrieks as they sway to the strength of the north winds.

A Good Time for Field Walks.--Nevertheless winter is a good time for the bird student to go afield. If the wild life is less abundant, so is the human life, and you have the country almost to yourself. If you but say in your heart, "I will go and see what may be {83} found," you will later rejoice, for with the falling of the leaves many of Nature's secrets, which she has jealously guarded through the summer months, stand revealed. Among the naked branches of the briars you may find the Catbird's nest which defied all search last June. It will be a comfort to learn that the bird really did have a nest just about the place you thought it was located. Many other pleasing surprises await you in the winter woods.

The Downy's Winter Quarters.--One late autumn day I stopped to watch a Junco feeding among some weed stalks near a hillside trail. After remaining motionless for a minute or two I became conscious of a light muffled tapping somewhere near by. It did not take long to locate the sound. On the underside of a slanting decayed limb, twenty feet above, was a new, well-rounded hole perhaps an inch in diameter. Even as I looked the occupant came to the entrance and threw out a billful of small chips. When these fell, I saw that the dead leaves on the earth beneath had been well sprinkled by previous ejections {84} of the same nature. I had discovered a Downy Woodpecker at work on his winter bedroom, and later I had reason to believe that he made this his nightly retreat during the cold months that followed.

Chancing to pass this way one dark cloudy morning, it occurred to me to look and see if he had yet left his bed. Striking the limb near the hole I was rewarded by seeing a little black-and-white head poked out inquiringly. Fearing he might be resentful if such treatment were repeated, I never afterward disturbed my little neighbour while he was taking his morning nap. But I had learned this much, that one Downy at least sometimes liked to be abed on cold mornings. Perhaps he knew that there was no early worm about at this season.

Birds and the Night.--It may be that others of our winter birds also make excavations for sleeping quarters; the Chickadee and Nuthatch very probably do so, although I have never found them thus engaged. It is well known that many small birds creep into holes to pass the night. Old nesting {85} places of Woodpeckers are thus again rendered useful, and many of the natural cavities of trees contain, during the hours of darkness, the little warm, pulsating bodies of birds.

Quails invariably roost on the ground regardless of the time of year, or the prevailing weather conditions. An entire covey numbering sometimes twelve or fifteen will settle for the night in a compact circular group with heads pointed outward. When a heavy snow falls they are completely buried, and then if a hard crust forms before morning their roosting place becomes their tomb. Grouse now and then are trapped in the same way, but their superior strength enables them to break through and escape. In fact, these larger birds often deliberately go to roost beneath the snow, breaking through the crust by a swift plunging dive from the air. Bearing these facts in mind it is easy to understand why Quails often become scarce in a country where Grouse abound.

Small birds pass the winter nights in evergreens, thick-growing vines, under the eaves of verandas, or {86} on the rafters of bridges. Many creep into cracks of outhouses. I have found them at night in caves, barns, and once in a covered wagon. Almost any available shelter may have its bird tenant on cold nights, who if undisturbed will often return again and again to the refuge it has once found safe and comfortable.

Birds that pass the winter in the Northern States are subjected to many hardships. In fact, the fatalities in the bird world in winter are so great, and the population so constantly reduced by one form of tragedy or another, that it is only the stronger and more fortunate individuals of a species that survive to enjoy the summer.

The Food Question in Winter.--Where to secure the food is the big question which confronts every bird when it opens its eyes on the first snowy morning of winter. Not only has the whole aspect of the country been changed, but the old sources of food have passed away. Not a caterpillar is to be found on the dead leaves, and not a winged insect is left to come flying {87} by; hence other food must be looked for in new directions. Emboldened by hunger, the Starlings alight at the kitchen door, and the Juncos, Sparrows, Downy Woodpeckers, and Nuthatches come to feed on the window-sill. Jays and Meadowlarks haunt the manure piles or haystacks in search of fragments of grain. Purple Finches flock to the wahoo elm trees to feed on the buds, and Crossbills attack the pine cones. Even the wary Ruffed Grouse will leave the shelter of the barren woods, and the farmer finds her in the morning sitting among the branches of his apple tree, relieving the twigs of their buds. In every field a multitude of weed stalks and stout grass stems are holding their heads above the snow tightly clasping their store of seeds until members of the Sparrow family shall thrash them out against the frozen crust beneath.

Among those which are forced to become largely vegetarian in winter is the Bluebird. In summer he is passionately fond of grasshoppers, cutworms, and Arctia caterpillars, but now he wanders sadly over {88} the country of his winter range in quest of the few berries to be found in the swamps and along the hedgerows. The Crow is another bird often met in winter walks, for he, too, in many cases spurns the popular movement southward in the fall, and severe indeed must be the weather before he forsakes his former haunts. You will find him feeding along the banks of streams or in the open spots in the fields, or {89} again in the woods pecking rotten stumps or fallen limbs in search of dormant beetles.

Fifty-five species of Warblers inhabit North America. These birds are insectivorous in their feeding habits, which of course also means that they are migratory. A partial exception to the rule is found in the common Myrtle Warbler. Although in winter these birds range south to Panama, many remain as far north as New Jersey, Kansas, and the Ohio Valley. This does not mean that insects are found in these regions in sufficient numbers to supply the larder of the Myrtle Warblers, but it does mean that they find acceptable substitutes for their usual food. Oddly enough, what they depend on is not animal matter in any form, but consists of berries which contain some of the essential food properties of fatty meats. One of the most popular with them is the common bayberry.

Among the sand dunes of the extensive "Banks" along the North Carolina coast there grows in great profusion a small bushy tree known as the yaupon. {90} The young leaves of this when dried and steeped make a very acceptable drink, and during the hungry days of the Civil War when the Federal blockade became effective the people of the region used this as a substitute for tea and coffee. The yaupon produces in great abundance a berry that is so highly esteemed by the Myrtle Warblers that they pass the winter in these regions in numbers almost incredible.

When the Food Supply Fails.--It is hard to realize the extent of the havoc wrought among birds by cold, snowy weather. Early in the year 1895 a long, severe cold spell, accompanied by snow and sleet, almost exterminated the Bluebird in the eastern United States. The bodies of no less than twenty-four of these birds were found in the cavity of one tree. It looked as if they had crowded together with the hope of keeping warm. It was not the cold alone which had destroyed the birds: a famine had preceded the cold snap, and the birds, weakened by hunger, were ill prepared to withstand its rigours.

One winter some years ago a prolonged freezing {91} wave swept over our South Atlantic States, and played havoc with the Woodcock in South Carolina. This is what happened: the swamps in the upper reaches of the Pee Dee, the Black, and Waccamaw rivers were frozen solid, and the Woodcock, that in winter abound in this region, were thus driven to the softer grounds farther downstream. The cold continued and the frozen area followed the birds. The Woodcock, unable to drive their long bills into the once-responsive mud, were forced to continue their flight toward the coast in search of open ground where worms could be found. When at length they reached Winyaw Bay, where these rivers converge, they were at the point of exhaustion. Thousands of the emaciated birds swarmed in the streets and gardens of Georgetown. They were too weak to fly, and negroes killed them with sticks and offered baskets of these wasted bodies, now worthless as food, for a few cents a dozen. Several shipments were made to Northern cities by local market men, who hoped to realize something by their industry.

Of the Wild Ducks which remain North in the winter many die because of the freezing of the water in which they must dive or dabble for their food. On the morning of February 11, 1912, Cayuga Lake in western New York State was found to be covered with a solid sheet of ice from end to end. It is a large body of water, having an area of nearly sixty-seven square miles. It rarely freezes over--only once in about twenty years, as the records show. The Ducks inhabiting the lake at this time were caught unawares. Many of them moved quickly to more Southern waters, but others tarried, evidently hoping for better times. Subsequently a few air-holes opened and the Ducks gathered about them, but there was little food even here, and numbers starved to death. One observer who went out to the air-holes reported examining the bodies of twenty-eight Canvas-backs and nineteen Scaups in addition to many others such as Redheads and Golden-eyes. His survey was not exhaustive and the Gulls had doubtless removed many bodies from the territory {93} he visited. When the surface of lakes and bays freezes suddenly in the night Ducks are sometimes caught and held fast by the ice adhering to their feathers and legs. In this condition they are utterly unable to escape the attacks of man and beast, and in the latitude of New York captures in this way are now and then reported.

Wild Fowl Destroyed in the Oil Fields.--In the oil fields of the Southwest and old Mexico the surface of many ponds is covered with oil into which unsuspecting flocks of Ducks alight never again to emerge until their dead bodies drift to the shore. It was on November 27, 1912, that the naval tank ship Arethusa steamed into the harbour of Providence, Rhode Island, with a cargo of crude oil. For several days following her bilge pumps sent overboard a continuous stream of water and oil seepage. On December 3d the following news-item appeared in the Providence Daily Bulletin, "The east shore of the lower harbour and upper bay, from Wilkesbarre pier to Riverside and below, is strewn with the bodies of dead {94} Wild Ducks, which began to drift ashore yesterday. The wildfowl came into the bay in enormous flocks about the middle of November and have since been seen flying about or feeding in the shallow water, as is usual at this time of year. As no such amount of oil, it is believed, was ever let loose into the bay at one time before, and as Ducks along the shore, dead from poisoning, have never been seen before, it is reasonable to connect the two occurrences."

Hunting Winter Birds.--Birds are to be found in winter in nearly every neighbourhood, and it is astonishing under what adverse natural conditions one may find them. As I write these lines on a dark February afternoon, here in New York City, I can see through the window a Starling sitting ruffled up on the bare twig of an elm tree. Every minute or two he calls, and as he is looking this way perhaps he is growing impatient for the little girl of the house to give him his daily supply of crumbs. A few minutes ago there was a Downy on the trunk of the same tree, and out over the Harlem River I see a flock of {95} Herring Gulls passing, as their custom is in the late afternoon.

Several years ago Dr. Frank M. Chapman sent out a notice to bird students that he would be pleased to have them make a record of the birds to be seen in their different neighbourhoods on Christmas.

Many responded, and he published their reports in his magazine Bird-Lore. This aroused so much interest that bird observers all over the country now have a regular custom of following this practice. In the January-February, 1916, issue of Bird-Lore appears the results of the last census which was taken on December 25, 1915. By examining this one may get a good idea of the birds to be found in various communities at this season. Some of the lists were very large, ninety-three specimens being noted in the one sent by Ludlow Griscom, from St. Marks, Florida. The largest number reported by any of the observers was 221, seen in the neighbourhood of Los Angeles, California. The following are reports from typical sections:

Wolfville, N. S.--Dec. 25; 10 A. M. to 12.30 P. M. Cloudless; 5 inches of light snow; no wind; temperature 30 degrees. Herring Gull, 2; Black Duck, 100; Canada Ruffed Grouse, 4; Downy Woodpecker, 1; Northern Raven, 1; Crow, 6; Goldfinch, 11; Vesper Sparrow, 1 (collected for positive identification); Black-capped Chickadee, 7; Acadian Chickadee, 2; Golden-crowned Kinglet, 5. Total, 11 species, 140 individuals. Dec. 20, a flock of 8 to 10 American Crossbills.--R. W. TUFTS.

Tilton, N. H.--Dec. 25; 8.20 A. M. to 12.30 P. M. Cloudy, changing to light rain; a little snow on ground; wind light, south-east; temperature 38 degrees. Blue Jay, 1; White-breasted Nuthatch, 1; Chickadee, 6; Golden-crowned Kinglet, 2.

Total, 4 species, 10 individuals. Birds seem unusually scarce this winter.-- GEORGE L. PLIMPTON and EDWARD H. PERKINS.

Bridgewater, Mass.--Dec. 25; 8 to 10 A. M. Cloudy; ground bare; wind southeast, moderate; temperature 27 degrees to 42 degrees. Red-tailed Hawk, 2; Northern Flicker, 3; Blue Jay, 3; American Crow, 80; Starling, 6; Meadowlark, 2; Goldfinch, 7; Junco, 5; Song Sparrow, 42; Swamp Sparrow, 2; Myrtle Warbler, 50; Brown Creeper, 2; Chickadee, 50; Golden-crowned Kinglet, 3. Total, 14 species, 256 individuals.--HORACE A. MCFARLIN.

Fairfield, Conn. (Birdcraft Sanctuary, 10 acres).--Dec. 25, Herring Gull, 4; Red-tailed Hawk, 2; Sparrow Hawk, 1; Hairy Woodpecker, 1; Downy Woodpecker, 5; Blue Jay, 4; Crow, 8; Starling, flock of 50; Meadowlark, 2; Purple Finch, 10; Goldfinch, 3; White-throated Sparrow, 4; Tree Sparrow, 15; Junco, 30; Song Sparrow, 7; Fox Sparrow, 1; Myrtle Warbler, 12; Brown Creeper, 3; White-breasted Nuthatch, 2; Chickadee, 10; Golden-crowned Kinglet, 5; Robin, 2. Total, 22 species, 181 individuals.--FRANK NOVAK, Warden.

New York City (Central Park).--Dec. 25; 9 A. M. to 1 P. M. Cloudy; ground mostly bare, with some remaining patches of snow; wind southeast, light; temperature 45 degrees to 54 degrees. Herring Gull, 70; Black Duck, 1; Downy Woodpecker, 2; Starling, 24; Junco, 4; Song Sparrow, 2; Cardinal, 2; Chickadee, 5. Total, 8 species, 110 individuals.--MR. and MRS. G. CLYDE FISHER.

Rhinebeck, N. Y.--Dec. 25; 8 A. M. to 1 P. M. Cloudy; deep snow; wind south, light; temperature 40 degrees. American Merganser, 2; Ring-necked Pheasant, 30; Gray Partridge, 5; Marsh Hawk, 1; Barred Owl, 1; Hairy Woodpecker, 4; Downy Woodpecker, 8 (drums and utters long call); yellow-bellied Sapsucker, 1 male; Blue Jay, 10; Crow, 15; Purple Finch, 15; Goldfinch, 6; Junco, 12; Song Sparrow, 1; Tree Sparrow, 13; Brown Creeper, 3; White-breasted Nuthatch, 20; Chickadee, 25 (whistles). Total 18 species, 171 individuals.--MRS. J. F. GOODWELL, TRACY, DOWS, and MAUNSELL S. CROSBY.

Hackettstown, N. J.--Dec. 22; 8.30 to 10.45 A. M. and 2.15 to 4.50 P. M. Fair; remains of 16 in. snow, ground partly bare, partly with deep drifts; temperature 20 degrees. Pheasant, 2; Sparrow Hawk, 1; Downy Woodpecker,

4; Blue Jay, 1; Crow, 4; Starling, 11; Meadowlark, 13; Goldfinch, 1; Tree Sparrow, 6; Junco, 14; Song Sparrow, 3; Brown Creeper, 2; White-breasted Nuthatch, 2; Chickadee, 11; Golden-crowned Kinglet, 1; Robin, 1; Bluebird, 2. Total, 17 species, 79 individuals.--MARY PIERSON ALLEN.

Doylestown, Pa.--Dec. 25; 10 A. M. to 2.30 P. M. Fair; ground snow-covered; wind southwest; temperature 40 degrees. Red-shouldered Hawk, 1; Sparrow Hawk, 1; Hairy Woodpecker, 1; Downy Woodpecker, 3; Blue Jay, 5; Crow, 7; Starling, 10; Meadowlark, 3; Purple Finch, 3; Tree Sparrow, 8; Junco, 42; Song Sparrow, 4; Cardinal, 2; White-breasted Nuthatch, 3; Tufted Titmouse, 5; Black-capped Chickadee, 16; Robin, 1; Bluebird, 2. Total, 18 species, 117 individuals--DOYLESTOWN NATURE CLUB, per Miss ELIZABETH COX.

Lexington, N. C.--Dec. 27; 9.30 A. M. to 4.30 P. M. Fair to hazy; ground bare; wind southeast to south, light; temperature 44 degrees to 50 degrees. Mourning Dove, 1; Turkey Vulture, 21; Sparrow Hawk, 1; Downy Woodpecker, 1; Yellow-bellied Sapsucker, 2; Northern Flicker, 9; Blue Jay, 12; Crow, 15; Purple Finch, 10; Goldfinch, 13; White-throated Sparrow, 50; Chipping Sparrow, 15; Field Sparrow, 30; Slate-coloured Junco, 100; Song Sparrow, 26; Fox Sparrow, 2; Towhee, 4; Cardinal, 20; {98} Mockingbird, 5; Carolina Wren, 12; House Wren, 2; Long-billed Marsh Wren, 1; White-breasted Nuthatch, 4; Tufted Titmouse, 4; Carolina Chickadee, 20; Golden-crowned Kinglet, 3; Bluebird, 8. Total, 27 species, 391 individuals.--THEODORE ANDREWS.

Columbia, S. C. (Outskirts).--Dec. 27; 11 A. M. to 1 P. M. Clear; ground bare; wind southwest, light; temperature 47 degrees. Black Vulture, 30; Red-tailed Hawk, 2; Red-headed Woodpecker, 6; Flicker, 1; Blue Jay, 12; Goldfinch, 7; White-throated Sparrow, 15; Slate-coloured Junco, 35; Song Sparrow, 6; Red-eyed Towhee, 3; Loggerhead Shrike, 1; Mockingbird, 3; Carolina Wren, 7; Brown Creeper, 1; Carolina Chickadee, 8; Golden-crowned Kinglet, 2; Ruby-crowned Kinglet, 8. Total, 17 species, 147 individuals.--BELLE WILLIAMS.

Tampa, Fla.--Dec. 26; 9 A. M. to 12 M. and 2 to 5 P. M. Clear; wind northwest, steady; tide out all day; temperature 40 degrees. Laughing Gull, 1; Bonaparte's Gull, 1; Brown Pelican, 9; Lesser Scaup, 75; Ward's Heron, 2; Little Blue Heron, 5; Killdeer, 15; Mourning Dove, 3; Turkey Vulture, 10; Black Vulture, 4; Marsh Hawk, 1; Bald Eagle, 1; Kingfisher, 1; Red-headed Woodpecker, 1; Florida Blue Jay, 5; Towhee, 1; Tree Sparrow, 14; Loggerhead

Shrike, 6; Myrtle Warbler, 20; Yellow-throated Warbler, 1; Palm Warbler, 60; Prairie Warbler, 1; Mockingbird, 12; House Wren, 2; Ruby-crowned Kinglet, 2; Blue-gray Gnatcatcher, 3. Total, 26 species, about 360 individuals.--MRS. HERBERT R. MILLS.

Rantoul, Ill.--Dec. 25; 11 A. M. to 2 P. M. Cloudy; wind north-west, strong; temperature 22 degrees. Prairie Hen, 40; Mourning Dove, 2; Cooper's Hawk, 2; Red-tailed Hawk, 1; Red-shouldered Hawk, 1; American Rough-legged Hawk, 5; American Sparrow Hawk, 1; Short-eared Owl, 3; Screech Owl, 1; Northern Downy Woodpecker, 5; Yellow-bellied Sapsucker, 2; Northern Flicker, 2; Horned Lark, 60; Prairie Horned Lark, 30; Blue Jay, 15; Bronzed Crackle, 2; Lapland Longspur, 4; Tree Sparrow, 200; Junco, 100; Song Sparrow, 8; Swamp Sparrow, 2; Cardinal, 16; Brown Creeper, 1; White-breasted Nuthatch, 10; Red-breasted Nuthatch, 4; Tufted Titmouse, 30; Chickadee, 24; {99} Golden-crowned Kinglet, 4. Total, 28 species, 575 individuals.--GEORGE E. EKBLAW and EDDIE L. EKBLAW.

Youngstown, Ohio.--Dec. 25; 8 A. M. to 4 P. M. Rain nearly all day; wind southerly, brisk at times; temperature 46 degrees to 33 degrees; walked about 10 miles. Ruffed Grouse, 2; Barred Owl, 1; Great Horned Owl, 2; Hairy Woodpecker, 6; Downy Woodpecker, 30; Red-bellied Woodpecker, 1; Blue Jay, 21; Goldfinch, 4; Tree Sparrow, 54; Slate-coloured Junco, 4; Song Sparrow, 20; Cardinal, 25; Winter Wren, 1; Brown Creeper, 4; White-breasted Nuthatch, 50; Red-breasted Nuthatch, 2; Tufted Titmouse, 25; Chickadee, 133; Golden-crowned Kinglet, 29; Wood Thrush, 1. Total, 20 species, 424 individuals. The Wood Thrush was possibly crippled, but could fly quite well.--GEORGE L. FORDYCE, VOLNEY ROGERS, C. A. LEEDY, and MRS. WILLIS H. WARNER.

Westfield, Wis.--Dec. 22; 8.30 to 10.30 A. M. Cloudy; ground covered by light snow; wind south, light; temperature 30 degrees. Ruffed Grouse, 1; Downy Woodpecker, 2; Blue Jay, 3; Goldfinch, 40; Tree Sparrow, 20; White-breasted Nuthatch, 3; Chickadee, 12. Total, 7 species, 81 individuals.--PATIENCE NESBITT.

Omaha, Neb.--Dec. 25; 10 A. M. to 3 P. M. Clear till noon; 1 inch of snow with bare spots; wind light, south; temperature 20 to 32 degrees. Open woods and parks just west of town, walked north 5 miles. Hairy Woodpecker, 1; Downy Woodpecker, 7; Blue Jay, 8; Goldfinch, 2; Pine Siskin, 1; Tree

Sparrow, 75; Slate-coloured Junco, 20; Cardinal, 2; White-breasted Nuthatch, 3; Chickadee, 26. Total, 10 species, 145 individuals.--SOLON R. TOWNE.

Denver, Colo.--Dec. 25; 2.20 to 4 P. M. Partly cloudy; ground with some snow; wind west, strong; temperature 45 degrees to 55 degrees. Ring-necked Pheasant, 11; Marsh Hawk, 1; Orange-shafted Flicker, 9; Magpie, 75; Red-winged Blackbird, 750; Meadowlark, 4; House Finch, 35; Tree Sparrow, 60; Shufeldt's Junco, 3; Pink-sided Junco, 1; Gray-headed Junco, 18. Total, 11 species, 967 individuals.--W. H. BERGTOLD.

Escondido, Calif.--Dec. 25; 9 A. M. to 2 P. M. Partly cloudy; {100} temperature 65 degrees. Killdeer, 30; Valley Quail, 100; Mourning Dove, 20; Western Red-tailed Hawk, 1; Desert Sparrow Hawk, 2; Barn Owl, 2; Burrowing Owl, 3; California Screech Owl, 1; Red-shafted Flicker, 3; Black-chinned Hummingbird, 3; Arkansas Kingbird, 9; Say's Phoebe, 4; Black Phoebe, 2; California Jay, 4; Western Meadowlark, 75; Brewer's Blackbird, 150; House Finch, 200; Willow Goldfinch, 50; Anthony's Towhee, 35; Phainopepla, 1; California Shrike, 8; Audubon's Warbler, 30; Western Mockingbird, 10; Pasadena Thrasher, 3; California Bush Tit, 20; Pallid Wren Tit, 6; Western Robin, 25; Western Bluebird, 10. Total, 38 species, 805 individuals.--FRED GALLUP.

CHAPTER VI

THE ECONOMIC VALUE OF BIRDS

Wild birds are now generally protected by law. Wander where you will through every province of Canada, and almost every nook and corner of the United States, you will find that the lawmaker has been there before you, and has thrown over the birds the sheltering arm of prohibitory statutes. Legislators are not usually supposed to spend much energy on drafting and enacting measures unless it is thought that these will result in practical benefit to at least some portion of their constituents. Legislative bodies are not much given to appropriating hundreds of thousands of dollars annually for the enforcement of a law which is purely sentimental in its nature. It is clear, therefore, that our law makers regard the wild bird life as {102} a great value to the country from the standpoint of dollars and cents.

Destructiveness of Insects.--If we go back a few years and examine certain widely read publications issued by the United States Department of Agriculture, we can understand more fully why our legislative bodies have regarded so seriously the subject of bird protection. In one of the Year Books of the Department we read that the annual loss to the cotton crop of the United States by insects amounts to sixty million dollars. We learn, too, that grasshoppers and other insects annually destroy fifty-three million dollars' worth of hay and that two million dollars' worth of cereals are each year eaten by our insect population. In fact, we are told that one-tenth of all the cereals, hay, cotton, tobacco, forests, and general farm products is the yearly tax which insects levy and collect. In some parts of the country market-gardening and fruit-growing are the chief industries of the people. Now, when a vegetable raiser or fruit grower starts to count up the cost of {103} his crops, one of the items which he must take into consideration is the 25 per cent. of his products which goes to feed the insects of the surrounding country.

Not all insects are detrimental to man's interests, but as we have just seen the Government officially states that many of them are tremendously destructive. Any one who has attempted to raise apples, for example, has made the unpleasant acquaintance of the codling moth and the curculio. Every season the apple raisers of the United States expend eight and one-quarter million dollars in spraying, to discourage the activities of these pests. In considering the troubles of the apple growers we may go even farther and count the twelve million dollars' worth of fruit spoiled by the insects despite all the spraying which has taken place. Chinch bugs destroy wheat to the value of twenty million dollars a year, and the cotton-boll weevil costs the Southern planters an equal amount.

Plagues of Insects.--Every now and then we read {104} of great plagues of insects which literally lay waste a whole section of country. History tells of these calamities which have troubled the civilized world from the days of Pharaoh to the present time. During the summer of 1912 there was a great outbreak of army worms in South Carolina. In innumerable millions they marched across the country, destroying vegetation like a consuming fire. In the year 1900 Hessian flies appeared in great numbers in Ohio and Indiana, and before they subsided they had destroyed absolutely two and one-half million acres of the finest wheat to be found in the Middle West, and wheat land dropped 40 per cent. in value.

Closing this Year Book, with its long tables of discouraging statements, we may find more cheerful reading if we turn to another Agricultural Department publication entitled, "Some Common Birds and Their Relation to Agriculture; Farmers Bulletin number Fifty-four." We need peruse only a few pages to become impressed with the fact that our Government Biological Survey has made an {105} exhaustive and exceedingly thorough investigation of the feeding habits of the wild birds that frequent the fields and forests. The reports of the economic ornithologists herein given are almost as surprising as the sad records given by the entomologists in the Year Book. We learn that birds, as a class, constitute a great natural check on the undue increase of harmful insects, and furthermore that the capacity for food of the average bird is decidedly greater in proportion than that of any other vertebrate.

Some Useful Birds.--Most people who have made the acquaintance of our common birds know the friendly little Chickadee, which winter and summer is a constant resident in groves of deciduous trees. It feeds, among other things, on borers living in the bark of trees, on plant lice which suck the sap, on caterpillars which consume the leaves, and on codling worms which destroy fruit. One naturalist found that four Chickadees had eaten one hundred and five female cankerworm moths. With scalpel, tweezers, and microscope these moths were examined, {106} and each was found to contain on an average one hundred and eighty-five eggs. This gives a total of nearly twenty thousand cankerworm moth eggs destroyed by four birds in a few minutes. The Chickadee is very fond of the eggs of this moth and hunts them assiduously during the four weeks of the summer when the moths are laying them.

The Nighthawk, which feeds mainly in the evening, and which is equally at home in the pine barrens of Florida, the prairies of Dakota, or the upper air of New York City, is a slaughterer of insects of many kinds. A Government agent collected one, in the stomach of which were the remains of thirty-four May beetles, the larvae of which are the white grubs well known to farmers on account of their destruction of potatoes and other vegetables. Several stomachs have been found to contain fifty or more different kinds of insects, and the number of individuals in some cases run into the thousands. Nighthawks also eat grasshoppers, potato-beetles, cucumber-beetles, boll-weevils, leaf-hoppers, and numerous gnats and {107} mosquitoes. Surely this splendid representative of the Goatsucker family deserves the gratitude of all American citizens.

Among the branches of certain of our fruit trees we sometimes see large webs which have been made by the tent caterpillars. An invading host seems to have pitched its tents among the boughs on all sides. If undisturbed these caterpillars strip the foliage from the trees. Fortunately there is a bird which is very fond of these hairy intruders. This is the Cuckoo, and he eats so many that his stomach actually becomes lined with a thick coating of hairs from their woolly bodies. The Baltimore Oriole also is fond of rifling these webs.

Another well-known bird that helps to make this part of the world habitable is the Flicker. It is popular in every neighbourhood where it is found and is known by a wide variety of local names, over one hundred and twenty-five of which have been recorded. Golden-winged Woodpecker some people call it. Other names are High-holder, Wake-up, {108} Walk-up, Yellowhammer, and Pigeon Woodpecker. The people of Cape Hatteras know it as Wilkrissen, and in some parts of Florida it is the Yucker-bird. Naturalists call it Colaptes auratus, but name it as you may, this bird of many aliases is well worthy of the esteem in which it is held. It gathers its food almost entirely from the ground, being different in this respect from other Woodpeckers. One may flush it in the grove, the forest, the peanut field, or the untilled prairie, and everywhere it is found engaged in the most highly satisfactory occupation of destroying insect life. More than half of its food consists of ants. In this country, taken as a whole, Flickers are very numerous, and the millions of individual birds which have yet escaped the guns of degenerate pot hunters constitute a mighty army of destruction to the Formicidae.

Let us not forget that any creature which eats ants is a decided boon to humanity. Ants, besides being wood borers, invaders of pantries, killers of young birds, nuisances to campers and barefoot {109} boys, care for and perpetuate plant lice which infest vegetation in all parts of the country to our very serious loss. Professor Forbes, in his study of the corn plant louse, found that in spring ants mine along the principal roots of the corn. Then they collect the plant lice, or aphids, and convey them into these burrows and there watch and protect them. Without the assistance of ants, it appears that the plant lice would be unable to reach the roots of the corn. In return for these attentions the ants feast upon the honey-like substances secreted by these aphids. The ants, which have the reputation of being no sluggards, take good care of their diminutive milch cattle, and will tenderly pick them up and transport them to new pastures when the old ones fail. Late in the summer they carefully collect all the aphid eggs that are obtainable, and taking them into their nests keep them safe during the winter. When spring comes and the eggs hatch, the ants gather the young plant lice and place them on plants. It may be seen, therefore, that the Flicker {110} by digging up ants' nests and feeding on the inhabitants has its value in an agricultural community.

The Question of the Weed Seeds.--The work of the Chickadee, the Nighthawk, the Cuckoo, and the Flicker is only an example of the good being done by at least two-thirds of birds in the United States, and most of the remainder are not without their beneficial qualities. When the coming of winter brings a cessation of insect life, many birds turn to the weed patches for food. Especially is this the case with the various varieties of native Sparrows.

No one has yet determined just how many weed seeds one of these birds will eat in a day. The number, however, must be very great. An ornithologist, upon examining the stomach of a Tree Sparrow, found it to contain seven hundred undigested pigeon-weed seeds, and in the same way it was discovered that a Snow Bunting had taken one thousand seeds of the pigweed at one meal.

Mr. E. H. Forbush, the well-known Massachusetts naturalist, frequently amuses himself by {111} observing the birds near his house as they feed on the millet seed that he provides for them. Speaking of some of the things he saw here, he says, "A Fox Sparrow ate one hundred and three seeds in two minutes and forty-seven seconds; another, one {112} hundred and ten in three minutes, forty-five seconds; while still another Song Sparrow ate one hundred and fifty-four in the same length of time. This Sparrow had been eating for half an hour before the count began and continued for some time after it was finished." It is readily seen that thirty seeds a minute was below the average of these birds; and if each bird ate at that rate for but a single hour each day it would destroy eighteen hundred seeds a day, or twelve thousand six hundred a week. Some day the economic ornithologists under the leadership of Professor F. E. L. Beal, America's leading authority on the subject, may give us a full and exhaustive account of what the various birds do for us in the way of keeping down the great scourge of grass and weeds with which the farmers have to deal. In the meantime, however, we may bear in mind that enough evidence already has been accumulated to prove that as destroyers of noxious weed seeds the wild birds are of vast importance.

Dealing with the Rodent Pests.--In addition to {113} weeds and insects, there is yet another group of pests, some representatives of which may be found in every neighbourhood. It is composed of rabbits, ground squirrels, prairie dogs, mice, and the like. They all possess long front teeth for gnawing, and constitute the Order of Rodents. Some species destroy fruit trees by gnawing away the bark near the ground, others attack the grain stacked in the field or stored in the granary. As these little sharp-eyed creatures are chiefly nocturnal in their habits, we seldom see them; we see only the ruin they have wrought. In some of the American ports incoming vessels are systematically fumigated to kill the rats for fear they may bring with them the bubonic plague. In April, 1898, while engaged in field natural history work in Hyde County, North Carolina, I found the farms along the north shore of Matamuskeet Lake were overrun by swarms of large brown rats that burrowed in the ground everywhere, and coming out at night wrought havoc and destruction on the farm lands. The whole country was up {114} in arms and the farmers were appealing for State and Federal aid to help them rid the land of this terrible scourge. In short, the rodents, as a class, are regarded as decidedly detrimental to the interests of mankind.

The Terror That Flies by Night.--Among the chief enemies of rodents in North America are the nineteen species of Owls, untold numbers of which are abroad every night searching through fields and forests for just such creatures as these. The digestive processes of Owls are such that the hard, indigestible portions of their food are disgorged in the form of balls and may often be found beneath their roosting places. One of our most odd-looking birds is the Barn Owl. Being nocturnal in its habits it is rarely seen unless one takes the trouble to climb into unfrequented church towers, the attics of abandoned buildings, or similar places which they seek out for roosting purposes. Some years ago the naturalist, Dr. A. K. Fisher, discovered that a pair of Barn Owls had taken up their abode in one of the towers {115} of the Smithsonion Institution building. He found the floor thickly strewn with pellets composed of bones and fur which these birds and their young had disgorged. He collected two hundred of these {116} and took them to his laboratory. A painstaking examination showed that they contained four hundred and fifty-three skulls. Here is his list made out at the time: two hundred and twenty-five meadow mice, two pine mice, twenty shrews, one star-nosed mole, and one Vesper Sparrow. It is plain to be seen that great good was accomplished in the community by this pair of Owls and their young, for the evil effects of the rodents in life must have far overbalanced the good service of the one useful Vesper Sparrow.

A Seldom Recognised Blessing.--There are some large predatory birds which destroy the lives of many game birds and others of the weaker species. On game farms, therefore, an unpleasant but necessary task is the shooting or trapping of Hawks and Owls. At first thought it might seem best to wage a war of absolute extermination on these offenders, and some game-keepers urge that this should be done. Personally I am opposed to any such course of action, one reason being that this would not {117} necessarily forward the best interests of the game birds it is desired to serve. So important and yet so unexpected is the ultimate effect of the activities of predatory creatures that in a state of nature I am convinced the supply of game birds is increased rather than decreased by being preyed upon. Like all other creatures, birds are subject to sickness and disease, but by the laws of nature it appears that they are not designed to suffer long. Their quick removal is advisable if they are to be prevented from spreading contagion among their fellows, or breeding and passing on their weakness to their offspring. Sometimes the Hawk, dashing at a covey of game birds, may capture one of its strongest and healthiest members, but the chances are that the afflicted member, which is not so quick on the rise or is a little slower on the wing, is the one to be taken. Just as some savages are said to put to death the incompetent and unfit, so do the laws operate which govern wild life. If, therefore, we should destroy all the Hawks, Owls, wild cats, foxes, skunks, {118} snakes, and other predatory creatures, it is an open question whether in the long run our game birds would be the gainers thereby.

Some time ago I visited a large game farm in one of the Southern States, where for several years the owner had been engaged in raising English Ring-necked Pheasants. The gamekeeper stated that there were about six thousand of these brilliantly coloured birds on the preserve at that time. He also pointed with pride to an exhibit on the walls of a small house. An examination showed that the two sides and one end of this building were thickly decorated with the feet of Hawks, Crows, Owls, domestic cats, minks, weasels, and other creatures that were supposed to be the enemies of Pheasants. Two men were employed on the place to shoot and trap at all seasons, and the evidences of their industry were nailed up, to let all men see that the owner of the big game farm meant to allow no wild bird or animal to fatten on his game birds.

A year later I again visited the same preserve and {119} found great lamentation. More than five thousand Pheasants had been swept away by disease within a few weeks. Is it going too far to say that the gunmen and trappers had overdone their work? So few Hawks or Owls or foxes had been left to capture the birds first afflicted, that these had been permitted to associate with their kind and to pass on weakness and disease to their offspring until the general health tone of the whole Pheasant community had become lowered. In the end five-sixths of the birds had succumbed to the devastations of disease.

All birds have their part to play in the great economy of the earth, and it is a dangerous experiment to upset the balance of Nature.

CHAPTER VII

CIVILIZATION'S EFFECT ON THE BIRD SUPPLY

Twelve hundred kinds of wild birds have been positively identified in North America. About one-third of this number are called sub-species, or climatic varieties. To illustrate the meaning of "sub-species," it may be stated that in Texas the plumage of the Bob-White is lighter in colour than the plumage of the typical eastern Bob-White, which was first described to science; therefore, the Texas bird is known as a sub-species of the type. Distributed through North America are nineteen sub-species of the eastern Song Sparrow. These vary from the typical bird by differences in size and shades of marking. In a similar way there are nine climatic variations of Screech Owls, six Long-billed Marsh Wrens, and fourteen Horned Larks. It is {121} difficult to explain why this variation in colour and size is so pronounced in some species and yet is totally absent in others of equally wide range. The Mourning Dove breeds in many localities from the southern tier of Canadian Provinces southward throughout the United States and Mexico, and yet everywhere over this vast range the birds are the same in size and colour. Nowhere do the individuals exhibit any markings suggestive of climatic influences.

Some birds are very rare and are admitted to the list of North American species because of the fact that during the years a few stragglers from other parts of the world have been found on our continent. Thus the Scarlet Ibis from South America, and the Kestrel and Rook from western Europe, are known to come to our shores only as rare wanderers who had lost their way, or were blown hither by storms. Eighty-five species of the birds now listed for North America are of this extra-limital class. Among those naturally inhabiting the country, some are, of course, much more abundant than others, thus every one {122} knows that Bald Eagles are comparatively rare, and that Robins and Chipping Sparrows exist by millions.

The Number of Birds in Different States.--The number of kinds of birds found in any one State depends on the size of the State, its geographical situation, and the varieties of its climate as affected by the topography in reference to mountains, coastlines, etc. The number of bird students and the character of their field studies determine the extent to which the birds of a State have been catalogued and listed. The following list indicates the number of kinds of birds that have been recorded in forty-three of the States and the District of Columbia. The authority for the statement in each instance and the year in which the figures were given is also stated:

Alabama, 275 (Oberholser, 1909). Arizona, 371 (Cooke, 1914). Arkansas, 255 (Howell, 1911). California, 541 (Grinnell, 1916). Colorado, 403 (Cooke, 1912). {123} Connecticut, 334 (Sage and Bishop, 1913). Delaware, 229 (Rennock, 1908). District of Columbia, 293 (Cooke, 1913). Florida, 362 (Thurston, 1916). Idaho, 210 (Merrill, 1898). Illinois, 390 (Cory, 1909). Indiana, 321 (Butler, 1898). Iowa, 356 (Anderson, 1907). Kansas, 379 (Bunker, 1913). Kentucky, 228 (Garman, 1894). Louisiana, 323 (Byer, Allison, Kopman, 1915). Maine, 327 (Knight, 1908). Maryland, 290 (Kirkwood, 1895). Massachusetts, 369 (Howe and Allen, 1901). Michigan, 326 (Barrows, 1912). Minnesota, 304 (Hatch, 1892). Missouri, 383 (Widmann, 1907). Nebraska, 418 (Swenk, 1915). Nevada, 250 (Hoffman, 1881). New Hampshire, 283 (Allen, 1904). New Jersey, 358 (Stone, 1916).

New Mexico, 314 (Ford, 1911). New York, 412 (Eaton, 1914). North Carolina, 342 (Pearson and Brimley, '16). North Dakota, 338 (Schmidt, 1904). Ohio, 330 (Jones, 1916). Oregon, 328 (Woodcock, 1902). Pennsylvania, 300 (Warren, 1890). Rhode Island, 293 (Howe and Sturtevant, 1899). South Carolina, 337 (Wayne, 1910). Tennessee, 223 (Rhoads, 1896). Texas, 546 (Strecker, 1912). Utah, 214 (Henshaw, 1874). Vermont, 255 (Howe, 1902). Virginia, 302 (Rives, 1890). Wellington, 372 (Dawson, 1909). West Virginia, 246 (Brooks, 1913). Wisconsin, 357 (Kumlien and Hollister, 1903). Wyoming, 288 (Knight, 1902).

For the five remaining States no list of the birds has as yet been issued.

Increase of Garden and Farm Birds.--The effect of civilization on the bird life of North America has been both pronounced and varied in character. Ask almost any one over fifty years of age if there are as many birds about the country as there were when he was a boy, and invariably he will answer "No!" This reply will be made, not because all birds have decreased in numbers, but because there has come a change in the man's ideas and viewpoint; in short, the change is chiefly a psychological one. The gentleman doubtless does not see the birds as much as he did when he was a boy on a farm, or if he does, they do not make the same impression on his mind. It is but another example of the human tendency to regard all things as better in the "good old times." Let us turn then from such well-meant but inaccurate testimony, and face the facts as they exist. I have no hesitation in saying that with many species of Finches, Warblers, Thrushes, and Wrens, their numbers in North America have greatly increased since the first coming of the white men to our shores.

It is a fact well known to careful observers that the deep, unbroken forests do not hold the abundance of bird life that is to be found in a country of farmlands, interspersed with thickets and groves. Originally extensive regions of eastern North America were covered with forests wherein birds that thrive in open countries could not find suitable habitation. As soon as the trees were cut the face of the country began to assume an aspect which greatly favoured such species as the Bobolink, Meadowlark, Quail, Vesper Sparrow, and others of the field-loving varieties. The open country brought them suitable places to nest, and agriculture increased their food supply. The settlers began killing off the wolves, wild cats, skunks, opossums, snakes, and many of the predatory Hawks, thus reducing the numbers of natural enemies with which this class of birds has to contend.

When the swamp is drained it means that the otter, the mink, and the Wild Duck must go, but the meadowland that takes the place of the swamp {127} provides for an increased number of other species of wild life.

Effect of Forest Devastation.--Only in a comparatively few cases has bird life suffered from the destruction of forests. In parts of the Middle West the Woodpeckers have no doubt decreased in {128} numbers. There are places where one may travel for many miles without seeing a single grove in which these birds could live.

Passenger Pigeons as late as 1870 were frequently seen in enormous flocks. Their numbers during the periods of migration was one of the greatest ornithological wonders of the world. Now the birds are gone. What is supposed to have been the last one died in captivity in the Zoological Park of Cincinnati at 2 P. M. on the afternoon of September 1, 1914. Despite the generally accepted statement that these birds succumbed to the guns, snares, and nets of hunters, there is a second cause which doubtless had its effect in hastening the disappearance of the species. The cutting away of vast forests where the birds were accustomed to gather and feed on mast greatly restricted their feeding range. They collected in enormous colonies for the purpose of rearing their young, and after the forests of the Northern States were so largely destroyed the birds seem to have been driven far up into Canada, quite {129} beyond their usual breeding range. Here, as Forbush suggests, the summer probably was not sufficiently long to enable them to rear their young successfully.

The Ivory-billed Woodpecker, the largest member of the Woodpecker family found in the United States, is now nearly extinct. There are some in the wilder regions of Florida, and a few in the swamps of upper Louisiana, but nowhere does the bird exist in numbers. It has been thought by some naturalists that the reduction of the forest areas was responsible for this bird's disappearance, but it is hard to believe that this fact alone was sufficient to affect them so seriously, for the birds live mainly in swamps, and in our Southern States there are extensive lowland regions that remain practically untouched by the axeman. For some reason, however, the birds have been unable to withstand the advance of civilization, and like the

Paroquet, the disappearance of which is almost equally difficult to explain, it will soon be numbered with the lengthening list of species that have passed away.

The Commercializing of Birds.--With the exceptions noted above the birds that have noticeably decreased in numbers in North America are those on whose heads a price has been set by the markets. Let a demand once arise for the bodies or the feathers of a species, and immediately a war is begun upon it that, unless speedily checked, spells disaster for the unfortunate bird.

The Labrador Duck and Others.--A hundred years ago the Labrador Duck, known to Audubon as the "Pied Duck," was abundant in the waters of the North Atlantic, and it was hunted and shot regularly in fall, winter, and spring, along the coast of New England and New York. Their breeding grounds were chiefly on the islands and along the shores of Labrador, as well as on the islands and mainland about the Gulf of St. Lawrence. Any one over forty years of age will remember how very popular feather beds used to be. In fact, there are those of us who know from experience that in many rural sections the deep feather bed is still regarded as the pi 鑓 e de {131} resistance of the careful householder's equipment. There was a time when the domestic poultry of New England did not furnish as great a supply of feathers as was desired. Furthermore, "Eider down" was recognized as the most desirable of all feathers for certain domestic uses.

A hundred and fifty years ago New England sea-faring men frequently fitted out vessels and sailed to the Labrador coast in summer on "feather-voyages." The feathers sought were those of the Labrador Duck and the Eider. These adventurous bird pirates secured their booty either by killing the birds or taking the down from the nests. The commercializing of the Labrador Duck meant its undoing. The last one known to have been taken was killed by a hunter near Long Island, New York, in 1875. Forty-two of these birds only are preserved in the ornithological collections of the whole world.

Another species which succumbed to the persistent persecution of mankind was the Great Cormorant that at one time was extremely abundant in the {132} northern Pacific and Bering Sea. They were killed for food by Indians, whalers, and others who visited the regions where the birds spend the summer. The Great Cormorant has been extinct in those waters since the year 1850.

Great Auks were once numbered literally by millions in the North Atlantic. They were flightless and exceedingly fat. They were easily killed with clubs on the breeding rookeries, and provided an acceptable meat supply for fishermen and other toilers of the sea; also their feathers were sought. They were very common off Labrador and Newfoundland. Funk Island, especially, contained an enormous breeding colony.

For years fishermen going to the Banks in early summer depended on Auks for their meat supply. The birds probably bred as far south as Massachusetts, where it is known a great many were killed by Indians during certain seasons of the year. However, it was the white man who brought ruin to this magnificent sea-fowl, for the savage Indians were {133} too provident to exterminate any species of bird or animal. The Great Auk was last seen in America between 1830 and 1840, and the final individual, so far as there is any positive record, was killed off Iceland in 1841. About eighty specimens of this bird, and seventy eggs, are preserved in the Natural History collections of the world.

The Trumpeter Swan and the Whooping Crane are nearly extinct to-day. Constant shooting and {134} the extensive settling of the prairies of the Northwest have been the causes of their disappearance.

Diminution of Other Species.--Of the fifty-five kinds of Wild Ducks, Geese, and Swans commonly found in North America, there is probably not one as numerous to-day as it was a hundred or even fifty years ago. Why? The markets where their bodies commanded a price of so much per head have swallowed them up. The shotgun has also played havoc with the Prairie Chicken and the Sage Grouse. Of the former possibly as many as one thousand exist on the Heath Hen Reservation of Martha's Vineyard, Massachusetts, a pitiful remnant of the eastern form of the species. Even in the Prairie States wide ranges of country that formerly knew them by tens of thousands now know them no more.

We might go farther and note also the rapidly decreasing numbers of the Sandhill Crane and the Limpkin of Florida. They are being shot for food. The large White Egret, the Snowy Egret, and the Roseate Spoonbill are found in lessening numbers each {135} year because they have been commercialized. There is a demand in the feather trade which can be met only by the use of their plumage, and as no profitable means has been devised for raising these birds in captivity the few remaining wild ones must be sacrificed, for from the standpoint of the killers it is better that a few men should become enriched by bird slaughter than that many people should derive pleasure from the birds which add so much beauty and interest to the landscape.

Change of Nesting Habits.--The nesting habits of some birds have been revolutionized by the coming of civilization to the American wilderness. The Swallow family provides three notable examples of this. The Cliff Swallow and Barn Swallow that formerly built their nests on exposed cliffs now seek the shelter of barns and other outbuildings for this purpose. The open nest of the Barn Swallow is usually found on the joists of hay barns and large stables and not infrequently on similar supports of wide verandas. The Cliff Swallow builds its gourd-shaped {136} mud nest under the eaves and hence is widely known as the Eaves Swallow. No rest of any kind in the form of a projecting beam is needed, as the bird skilfully fastens the mud to the vertical side of the barn close up under the overhanging roof. In such a situation it is usually safe from all beating rains. The Cliff Swallow has exhibited wisdom to no mean extent in exchanging the more or less exposed rocky ledge for the safety of sheltering eaves. Swallows show a decided tendency to gather in colonies in the breeding season. Under the eaves of a warehouse on the cost of Maine I once counted exactly one hundred nests of these birds, all of which appeared to be inhabited. Examination of another building less than seventy feet away added thirty-seven occupied nests to the list.

The nesting site of the Purple Martin has likewise been changed in a most radical fashion. Originally these birds built their nests of leaves, feathers, and grass, in hollow trees. Here no doubt they were often disturbed by weasels, squirrels, snakes, and {137} other consumers of birds and their eggs. Some of the southern Indians hung gourds up on poles and the Martins learned to build their nests in them. This custom is still in vogue in the South, and thousands of Martin houses throughout the country are erected every year for the accommodation of these interesting birds. By their cheerful twitterings and their vigilance in driving from the neighbourhood every Hawk and Crow that ventures near, they not only repay the slight effort made in their behalf, but endear themselves to the thrifty chicken-raising farm-wives of the country.

If gourds or boxes cannot be found Martins will sometimes build about the eaves of buildings or similar places. They have learned that it is wise to nest near human habitations. At Plant City, Florida, one may find their nests in the large electric arc-lights swinging in the streets, and at Clearwater, Florida, and in Bismarck, North Dakota, colonies nest under the projecting roofs of store buildings.

I have always been interested in finding nests of {138} birds, but I think no success in this line ever pleased me quite so much as the discovery of two pairs of Purple Martins making their nests one day in May, down on the edge of the Everglade country in south Florida. There were no bird boxes or gourds for at least twenty or thirty miles around, so the birds had appropriated some old Flicker nesting cavities in dead trees, that is, one pair of the birds had appropriated a disused hole, and the second pair was busy trying to carry nesting material into a Flicker's nest from which the young birds had not yet departed. Here then were Martins preparing to carry on their domestic duties just as they did back in the old primeval days.

The discussion of this subject could not well be closed without mentioning the Chimney Swift that now almost universally glues to the inner side of a chimney, or more rarely the inner wall of some building, the few little twigs that constitute its nest. It is only in the remotest parts of the country that these birds still resort to hollow trees for nesting purposes. {139} There is--or was a few years ago--a hollow cypress tree standing on the edge of Big Lake in North Carolina which was used by a pair of Chimney Swifts, and it made one feel as if he were living in primitive times to see these little dark birds dart downward into a hollow tree, miles and miles away from any friendly chimney. Some day I hope to revisit the region and find this natural nesting hollow still occupied by a pair of unmodernized Swifts.

CHAPTER VIII

THE TRAFFIC IN FEATHERS

The traffic in the feathers of American birds for the millinery trade began to develop strongly about 1880 and assumed its greatest proportions during the next ten years. The wholesale milliners whose business and pleasure it was to supply these ornaments for women's hats naturally turned for their supply first to those species of birds most easily procured. Agents were soon going about the country looking for men to kill birds for their feathers, and circulars and hand bills offering attractive prices for feathers of various kinds were mailed broadcast. The first great onslaughts were made on the breeding colonies of sea birds along the Atlantic Coast. On Long Island there were some very large communities of Terns and these were {141} quickly raided. The old birds were shot down and the unattended young necessarily were left to starve. Along the coast of Massachusetts the sea birds suffered a like fate. Maine with its innumerable out-lying rocky islands was, as it is to-day, the chief nursery of the Herring Gulls and Common Terns of the North Atlantic. This fact was soon discovered and thousands were slaughtered every summer, their wings cut off, and their bodies left to rot among the nests on the rookeries.

War on the Sea Swallows.--During a period of seven years more than 500,000 Terns', or Sea Swallows', skins were collected in spring and summer in the sounds of North and South Carolina. These figures I compiled from the records and accounts given me by men who did the killing. Their method was to fit out small sailing vessels on which they could live comfortably and cruise for several weeks; in fact, they were usually out during the entire three months of the nesting period. That was the time of year that offered best rewards for such work, for then the birds' {142} feathers bore their brightest lustre, and the birds being assembled on their nesting grounds they could easily be shot in great numbers. After the birds were killed the custom was to skin them, wash off the blood stains with benzine, and dry the feathers with plaster of Paris. Arsenic was used for curing and preserving the skins. Men in this business became very skilful and rapid in their work, some being able to prepare as many as one hundred skins in a day.

Millinery agents from New York would sometimes take skinners with them and going to a favourable locality would employ local gunners to shoot the birds which they in turn would skin. In this way one New York woman with some assistants collected and brought back from Cobbs' Island, Virginia, 10,000 skins of the Least Tern in a single season.

In the swamps of Florida word was carried that the great millinery trade of the North was bidding high for the feathers of those plume birds which gave life and beauty even to its wildest regions. It was not long before the cypress fastnesses were echoing {143} to the roar of breech-loaders, and cries of agony and piles of torn feathers became common sounds and sights even in the remotest depths of the Everglades. What mattered it if the semi-tropical birds of exquisite plumage were swept from existence, if only the millinery trade might prosper!

The milliners were not content to collect their prey only in obscure and little-known regions, for a chance was seen to commercialize the small birds of the forests and fields. Warblers, Thrushes, Wrens, in fact all those small forms of dainty bird life which come about the home to cheer the hearts of men and women and gladden the eyes of little children, commanded a price if done to death and their pitiful remains shipped to New York.

Taxidermists, who made a business of securing birds and preparing their skins, found abundant opportunity to ply their trade. Never had the business of taxidermy been so profitable as in those days. For example, in the spring of 1882 some of the feather agents established themselves at points {144} on the New Jersey coast, and sent out word to residents of the region that they would buy the bodies of freshly killed birds of all kinds procurable. The various species of Terns, which were then abundant on the Jersey coast, offered the best opportunity {145} for profit, for not only were they found in vast numbers, but they were comparatively easy to shoot. Ten cents apiece was the price paid, and so lucrative a business did the shooting of these birds become that many baymen gave up their usual occupation of sailing pleasure parties and became gunners. These men often earned as much as one hundred dollars a week for their skill with the shotgun.

It is not surprising that at the end of the season a local observer reported: "One cannot help noticing now the scarcity of Terns on the New Jersey coast, and it is all owing to their merciless destruction." One might go further and give the sickening details of how the birds were swept from the mud flats about the mouth of the Mississippi and the innumerable shell lumps of the Chandeleurs and the Breton Island region; how the Great Lakes were bereft of their feathered life, and the swamps of the Kankakee were invaded; how the White Pelicans, Western Grebes, Caspian Terns, and California Gulls of the West were butchered and their skinned {146} bodies left in pyramids to fester in the sun. One might recount stories of Bluebirds and Robins shot on the very lawns of peaceful, bird-loving citizens of our Eastern States in order that the feathers might be spirited away to feed the insatiable appetite of the wholesale milliner dealers. Never have birds been worn in this country in such numbers as in those days. Ten or fifteen small song birds' skins were often sewed on a single hat!

What the Ladies Wore.--In 1886 Dr. Frank M. Chapman walked through the shopping district of New York City on his way home, two afternoons in succession, and carefully observed the feather decorations on the hats of the women he chanced to meet. The result of his observation, as reported to Forest and Stream, shows that he found in common use as millinery trimming many highly esteemed birds as the following list which he wrote down at the time will serve to show:

Robins, Thrushes, Bluebirds, Tanagers, Swallows, {147} Warblers, Waxwings, Bobolinks, Larks, Orioles, Doves, and Woodpeckers.

In all, the feathers of at least forty species were discernible.

In commenting on his trips of inspection, Doctor Chapman wrote: "It is evident that in proportion to the number of hats seen, the list of birds given is very small, for in most cases mutilation rendered identification impossible. Thus, while one afternoon seven hundred hats were counted and on them but twenty birds recognized, five hundred and forty-two were decorated with feathers of some kind. Of the one hundred and fifty-eight remaining, seventy-two were worn by young or middle-aged ladies, and eighty-six by ladies in mourning or elderly ladies."

This was a period when people seemed to go mad on the subject of wearing birds and feathers. They were used for feminine adornment in almost every conceivable fashion. Here are two quotations from New York daily papers of that time, only the names {148} of the ladies are changed: "Miss Jones looked extremely well in white with a whole nest of sparkling, scintillating birds in her hair which it would have puzzled an ornithologist to classify," and again: "Mrs. Robert Smith had her gown of unrelieved black looped up with black birds; and a winged creature, so dusky that it could have been intended for nothing but a Crow, reposed among the curls and braids of her hair."

Ah, those were the halcyon days of the feather trade! Now and then a voice cried out at the slaughter, or hands were raised at the sight of the horrible shambles, but there were no laws to prevent the killing nor was there any strong public sentiment to demand its cessation, while on the other hand more riches yet lay in store for the hunter and the merchant. There were no laws whatever to protect these birds, nor was there for a time any man of force to start a crusade against the evil.

The Story of the Egrets.--The most shameless blot on the history of America's treatment of the {149} wild birds is in connection with the White Egrets. It is from the backs of these birds that the "aigrettes" come, so often seen on the hats of the fashionable. Years ago, as a boy in Florida, I first had an opportunity to observe the methods employed by the feather hunters in collecting these aigrettes which are the nuptial plumes of the bird and are to be found on birds only in the spring. As a rare treat I was permitted to accept the invitation extended by a squirrel hunter to accompany him to the nesting haunts of a colony of these birds. Away we went in the gray dawn of a summer morning through the pine barrens of southern Florida until the heavy swamps of Horse Hammock were reached. I remember following with intense interest the description given by my companion of how these birds with magnificent snowy plumage would come flying in over the dark forest high in air and then volplane to the little pond where, in the heavily massed bushes, their nests were thickly clustered. With vivid distinctness he imitated the cackling notes of the {150} old birds as they settled on their nests, and the shrill cries of the little ones, as on unsteady legs they reached upward for their food.

Keen indeed was the disappointment that awaited me. With great care we approached the spot and with caution worked our way to the very edge of the pond. For many minutes we waited, but no life was visible about the buttonwood bushes which held the nests--no old birds like fragments of fleecy clouds came floating in over the dark canopy of cypress trees. My companion, wise in the ways of hunters, as well as the habits of birds, suspected something wrong and presently found nearby the body of an Egret lying on the ground, its back, from which the skin bearing the fatal aigrettes had been torn, raw and bloody. A little farther along we came to the remains of a second and then a third, and still farther on, a fourth. As we approached, we were warned of the proximity of each ghastly spectacle by the hideous buzzing of green flies swarming over the lifeless forms of the parent birds.

At one place, beneath a small palmetto bush, we found the body of an Egret which the hunters had overlooked. Falling to the ground sorely wounded, it had escaped its enemies by crawling to this hiding-place. Its appearance showed the suffering which it had endured. The ground was bare where in its death agonies it had beaten the earth with its wings. The feathers on the head and neck were raised and the bill was buried among the blood-clotted feathers of its breast. On the higher ground we discovered some straw and the embers of a campfire, giving evidence of the recent presence of the plume hunters. Examination of the nests over the pond revealed numerous young, many of which were now past suffering; others, however, were still alive and were faintly calling for food which the dead parents could never bring. Later inquiry developed the fact that the plumes taken from the backs of these parent birds were shipped to one of the large millinery houses in New York, where in due time they were placed on the market as "aigrettes," and of course {152} subsequently purchased and worn by fashionable women, as well as by young and old women of moderate incomes, who sacrifice much for this millinery luxury.

There were at that time to be found in Florida many hundreds of colonies of these beautiful birds, but their feathers commanded a large price and offered a most tempting inducement for local hunters to shoot them. Many of the men of the region were poor, and the rich harvest which awaited them was very inviting. At that time gunners received from seventy-five cents to one dollar and a quarter for the "scalp" of each bird, which ordinarily contained forty or more plume feathers. These birds were not confined to Florida, but in the breeding season were to be found in swampy regions of the Atlantic Coast as far north as New Jersey, some being discovered carrying sticks for their nests on Long Island.

Civilized nations to-day decry any method of warfare which results in the killing of women and children, but the story of the aigrette trade deals with the slaughter of innocents by the slow process of {153} starvation, a method which history shows has never been followed by even the most savage race of men dealing with their most hated enemies. This war of extermination which was carried forward unchecked for years could mean but one thing, namely, the rapid disappearance of the Egrets in the United States. As nesting birds, they have disappeared from New Jersey, Maryland, and Virginia, and also those States of the central Mississippi Valley where they were at one time to be found in great numbers.

Amateur Feather Hunters.--Quite aside from the professional millinery feather hunter there should be mentioned the criminal slaughter of birds which has been indulged in by individuals who have killed them for the uses of their own lady friends. I know one Brown Pelican colony which was visited by a tourist who shot four hundred of the big, harmless, inoffensive creatures in order to get a small strip of skin on either side of the body. He explained to his boatmen, who did the skinning for him, that he was curious to see if these strips of skin with their feathers would not {154} make an interesting coat for his wife. The birds killed were all caring for their young in the nests at the time he and his hirelings shot them.

There was a few years ago, in a Georgia city, an attorney who accepted the aigrette "scalps" of twenty-seven Egrets from a client who was unable to pay cash for a small service rendered. He told me he had much pleasure in distributing these among his lady friends. Another man went about the neighbourhood hunting male Baltimore Orioles until he had shot twelve, as he wanted his sisters to have six each for their Sunday hats. The Roseate Spoonbill of the Southern States was never extensively killed for the millinery trade, and yet to-day it is rapidly approaching extinction. The feathers begin to fade in a short time and for this reason have little commercial value, but the amateur Northern tourist feather hunter has not known this, or disregarded the fact, and has been the cause of the depletion of the species in the United States. Almost every one could cite instances similar to the above, for there are many people in the {155} United States who are guilty of taking part in the destruction of birds for millinery purposes. In addition to the feathers of American birds already mentioned the feathers of certain foreign species have been very much in demand.

Paradise Plumes--One of the most popular foreign feathers brought to this country is the Paradise. There are at least nine species of Paradise Birds found in New Guinea and surrounding regions that furnish this product. The males are adorned with long, curved delicate feathers which are gorgeously coloured. As in the case of all other wild birds there is no way of getting the feathers except by killing the owners. Much of this is done by natives who shoot them down with little arrows blown through long hollow reeds. The high price paid for these feathers has been the occasion of the almost total extinction of some of the species, as indicated by the decreased number of feathers offered at the famous annual London Feather Sales. Travellers in the regions inhabited by the birds speak of the {156} distressing effect of the continuous calls of the bereft females as they fly about in the forests during the mating season. As a high-priced adornment the Paradise is the one rival of the famous aigrette.

Maribou.--The Maribou which has been fashionable for a number of years past comes principally from the Maribou Stork of Africa. These white, fluffy, downlike feathers grow on the lower underpart of the body of the Maribou Stork. These birds are found in the more open parts of the country. Their food consists of such small forms of life as may readily be found in the savannas and marshes. To some extent they also feed like vultures on the remains of larger animals.

Pheasants.--The long tail feathers of Pheasants have been much in demand by the millinery trade during the past ten years. Although several species contribute to the supply, the majority are from the Chinese Pheasant, or a similar hybrid descendent known as the English Ring-necked Pheasant. Many of these feathers have been collected in Europe, {157} where the birds are extensively reared and shot on great game preserves; vast numbers, however, have come from China. Oddly enough in that country the birds were originally little disturbed by the natives, who seem not to care for meat. Then came the demand for feathers, and the birds have since been killed for this purpose to an appalling extent.

Numidie.--This popular hat decoration suddenly appeared on our market in great numbers a few years ago. It is taken from the Manchurian Eared Pheasant of northern China. Unless the demand for these feathers is overcome in some way there will undoubtedly come a day in the not-distant future when the name of this bird must be added to the lengthening list of species that have been sacrificed to the greed of the shortsightedness of man.

Goura.--The fashionable and expensive hat decoration which passes under the trade name of Goura consists of the slender feathers, usually four or five inches long with a greatly enlarged tip, that grows out fanlike along a line down the centre of the head {158} and nape of certain large Ground Pigeons that inhabit New Guinea and adjacent islands. Perhaps the best-known species is the Crowned Pigeon.

There is a special trade name for the feathers of almost every kind of bird known in the millinery business. Thus there is Coque for Black Cock, Cross Aigrettes for the little plumes of the Snowy Egret, and Eagle Quills from the wings not only of Eagles, but of Bustards, Pelicans, Albatrosses, Bush Turkeys, and even Turkey Buzzards. The feathers of Macaws in great numbers are used in the feather trade, as well as hundreds of thousands of Hummingbirds, and other bright-coloured birds of the tropics.

Women's Love for Feathers.--One of the most coveted and easily acquired feminine adornments has been feathers. At first these were probably taken almost wholly from birds killed for food, but later, when civilization became more complex and resourceful, millinery dealers searched the ends of the earth to supply the demands of discriminating women. The chief reason why it has been so difficult {160} to induce educated and cultivated women of this age to give up the heartless practice of wearing feathers seems to be the fact that the desire and necessity for adornment developed through the centuries has become so strong as to be really an inherent part of their natures. It is doubtful if many people realize how strong and all-powerful this desire for conforming to fashion in the matter of dress sits enthroned in the hearts of tens of thousands of good women.

There was a time when I thought that any woman with human instincts would give up the wearing of feathers at once upon being told of the barbaric cruelties involved in their acquisition. But I have learned to my amazement that such is not the case. Not long ago I received one of the shocks of my life. Somewhat over two years ago a young woman came to work in our office. I supposed she had never heard, except casually, of the great scourge of the millinery trade in feathers. Since that time, however, she has been in daily touch with all the important efforts made in this country and abroad to {161} legislate the traffic out of existence, to guard from the plume hunters the colonies of Egrets and other water birds, and to educate public sentiment to a proper appreciation of the importance of bird protection. She has typewritten a four-hundred-page book on birds and bird protection, has acknowledged the receipt of letters from the wardens telling of desperate rifle battles that they have had with poachers, and written letters to the widow of one of our agents shot to death while guarding a Florida bird rookery. In the heat of campaigns she has worked overtime and on holidays. I have never known a woman who laboured more conscientiously or was apparently more interested in the work. Frequently her eyes would open wide and she would express resentment when reports reached the office of the atrocities perpetrated on wild birds by the heartless agents of the feather trade. Recently she married and left us. Last week she called at the office, looking very beautiful and radiant. After a few moments' conversation she approached the subject which {162} evidently lay close to her heart. Indicating a cluster of paradise aigrettes kept in the office for exhibition purposes, she looked me straight in the face and in the most frank and guileless manner asked me to sell them to her for her new hat! The rest of the day I was of little service to the world.

What was the good of all the long years of unceasing effort to induce women to stop wearing bird feathers, if this was a fair example of results? Of all the women I knew, there was no one who had been in a position to learn more of the facts regarding bird slaughter than this one; yet it seems that it had never entered her mind to make a personal application of the lesson she had learned. The education and restraint of legislative enactments were all meant for other people.

Ostrich Feathers Are Desirable.--How is this deep-seated desire and demand for feathers to be met? Domestic fowls will in part supply it; but for the finer ornaments we must turn to the Ostrich, the only bird in the world which has been domesticated {163} exclusively for its feather product. These birds were formerly found wild in Arabia, southwestern Persia, and practically the whole of Africa. In diminishing numbers they are still to be met with in these regions, especially in the unsettled parts of Africa north of the Orange River. From early times the plumes of these avian giants have been in demand for head decorations, and for centuries the people of Asia and Africa killed the birds for this purpose. They were captured chiefly by means of pitfalls, for a long-legged bird which in full flight can cover twenty-five feet at a stride is not easily overtaken, even with the Arabs' finest steeds.

So far as there is any record, young Ostriches were first captured and enclosed with a view of rearing them for profit in the year 1857. This occurred in South Africa. During the years which have since elapsed, the raising of Ostriches and the exportation of their plumes has become one of the chief business enterprises of South Africa. Very naturally people in other parts of the world wished to engage in a {164} similar enterprise when they saw with what success the undertaking was crowned in the home country of the Ostrich. A few hundred fine breeding birds and a considerable number of eggs were purchased by adventurous spirits and exported, with the result that Ostrich farms soon sprang up in widely separated localities over the earth. The lawmakers of Cape Colony looked askance at these competitors and soon prohibited Ostrich exportation. Before these drastic measures were taken, however, a sufficient number of birds had been removed to other countries to assure the future growth of the industry in various regions of the world. It was in 1882 that these birds were first brought to the United States for breeding purposes. To-day there are Ostrich farms at Los Angeles, San Diego, and San Jos? California; Hot Springs, Arkansas; Jacksonville, Florida; Phoenix, Arizona, and elsewhere.

There is money to be made in the Ostrich business, for the wing and tail plumes of this bird are as popular to-day for human adornment as they were in the {165} days of Sheerkohf, the gorgeous lion of the mountain. Even low-grade feathers command a good price for use in the manufacture of boas, feather bands, trimming for doll's hats, and other secondary purposes. When the time comes for plucking the feathers, the Ostriches are driven one at a time into a V-shaped corral just large enough to admit the bird's body and the workman. Here a long, slender hood is slipped over his head and the wildest bird instantly becomes docile. Evidently he regards himself as effectively hidden and secure from all the terrors of earth. There is no pain whatever attached to the taking of Ostrich feathers, for they are merely clipped from the bird by means of scissors. A month or two later when the stubs of the quills have become dry they are readily picked from the wings without injury to the new feathers.

The Ostrich industry is good and it is worthy of encouragement. No woman need fear that she is aiding in any way the destruction of birds by wearing Ostrich plumes. There are many more of the birds {166} in the world to-day than there were when their domestication first began, and probably no wild African or Asiatic Ostriches are now shot or trapped for their plumes. The product seen in our stores all comes from strong, happy birds hatched and reared in captivity. Use of their feathers does not entail the sacrifice of life, nor does it cause the slightest suffering to the Ostrich; taking plumes from an Ostrich being no more painful to the bird than shearing is to a sheep and does not cause it half the alarm a sheep often exhibits at shearing time.

The call for feather finery rings so loudly in the hearts of women that it will probably never cease to be heard, and it is the Ostrich--the big, ungainly yet graceful Ostrich--which must supply the demand for high-grade feathers of the future.

CHAPTER IX

BIRD-PROTECTIVE LAWS AND THEIR ENFORCEMENT--HOW LAWS ARE MADE

Laws for the protection of wild birds and animals have been enacted in greater numbers in the United States than in any other country in the world. In a Government Bulletin on American Game Protection, Dr. T. S. Palmer states that the earliest game laws were probably the hunting privileges granted in 1629 by the West India Company to persons planting colonies in the New Netherlands, and the provisions granting the right of hunting in the Massachusetts Bay Colonial Ordinance of 1647. As soon as the United States Government was formed, in 1776, the various States began to make laws on the subject, and these have increased in numbers with the passing of years. For example, between the years 1901 to 1910, North {168} Carolina alone passed three hundred and six different game laws. As various forms of game birds or animals showed indications of decreasing in numbers new laws were called into existence in an attempt to conserve the supply for the benefit of the people. Not infrequently laws were passed offering bounties or otherwise encouraging the killing of wolves, pumas, and other predatory animals, or of birds regarded as injurious to growing crops or to poultry raising.

State laws intended primarily for the protection of wild life may be grouped as follows: (1) naming the time of the year when various kinds of game may be hunted; these hunting periods are called "open seasons." (2) The prohibition of certain methods formally employed in taking game, as, for example, netting, trapping, and shooting at night. (3) Prohibiting or regulating the sale of game. By destroying the market the incentive for much excessive killing is removed. (4) Bag limit; that is, indicating the number of birds or animals that may be shot in a day; for example, in Louisiana one may kill twenty-five {169} Ducks in a day, and in Arizona one may shoot two male deer in a season. (5) Providing protection at all seasons for useful birds not recognized as game species.

Definition of Game.--Game animals as defined today include bears, coons, deer, mountain sheep, caribou, cougars, musk oxen, white goats, rabbits, squirrels, opossums, wolves, antelopes, and moose. Game birds include Swans, Geese, Ducks, Rails, Coots, Woodcocks, Snipes, Plovers, Curlews, Wild Turkeys, Grouse, Pheasants, Partridges, and Quails. Sometimes other birds or animals have been regarded as game. Robins and Mourning Doves, for example, are still shot in some of the Southern States as game birds.

The Audubon Law.--Little was done in the way of securing laws for the benefit of song and insectivorous birds and birds of plumage until 1886, when the bird-protection committee of the American Ornithologists' Union drafted a bill for this specific purpose. This bill, besides extending protection to all useful {170} non-game birds, gave the first clear statutory terminology for defining "game birds." It also provided for the issuing of permits for the collecting of wild birds and their eggs for scientific purposes. The States of New York and Massachusetts that year adopted the law. Arkansas followed eleven years later, but it was not until the Audubon Society workers took up the subject in 1909 that any special headway was made in getting States to pass this measure. To-day it is on the statute books of all the States of the Union but eight, and is generally known as the Audubon Law.

Game Law Enforcement.--In all the States but Florida there are special State officers charged with enforcing the bird and game protective laws. Usually there is a Game Commission of three or more members whose duty it is to select an executive officer who in turn appoints game wardens throughout the State. These men in some cases are paid salaries, in others they receive only a per diem wage or receive certain fees for convictions. License {171} fees are usually required of hunters, and the moneys thus collected form the basis of a fund used for paying the wardens and meeting the other expenses incident to the game law enforcement.

The Lacey Law.--The Federal Government is taking a share of the responsibility in preserving the wild life of the Union.

On July 2, 1897, Congressman Lacey introduced in the House a bill to prohibit the export of big game from some of the Western States. In 1909 amendments were made to the Lacey Law, one of which prohibited the shipment of birds or parts thereof from a State in which they had been illegally killed, or from which it was illegal to ship them. The enforcement of this by Federal officers has been most efficacious in breaking up a great system of smuggling Quails, Grouse, Ducks, and other game birds.

Federal Migratory Bird Law.--Probably the most important game law as yet enacted in the United States is the one known as the Federal Migratory Game Law or the McLean Law. A somewhat {172} extended discussion of this important measure seems justifiable at this time.

When, in 1913, the first breath of autumn swept over the tule sloughs and reedy lakes of the North-west, the wild fowl and shore birds of that vast region rose in clouds, and by stages began to journey toward {173} their winter quarters beneath Southern skies. If the older birds that had often taken the same trip thought anything about the subject, they must have been impressed, when they crossed the border into the United States, with the fact that changes had taken place in reference to shooting.

It is true that in Minnesota, for instance, the firing of guns began in September, as in other years; but those Ducks that reached the Mississippi River below St. Paul found no one waiting to kill them. As they proceeded, by occasional flights, farther down the river there was still a marked absence of gunners. The same conditions prevailed all the way down the valley until the sunken grounds of Arkansas and Mississippi came into view. What did this mean? Heretofore, at this season, hunters had always lined the river. This had been the case ever since the oldest Duck could remember. The Missouri River, too, was free from shooting throughout the greater part of its length, which was sufficient cause for many a grateful quack.

What was the reason for this great change? Had the killing of wild fowl suddenly lost its attraction for those who had been accustomed to seek pleasure afield with gun and decoys? No, indeed, banish the thought, for it is written that so long as man shall live, Wild Duck shall grace his table and gratify his palate.

The remarkable changes which had so affected the fortunes of the wild fowl were due to the enactment of a United States law known as the Federal Migratory Game Law. Let us see something of this law and of what led to its establishment.

History of Game Laws.--When the United States of America became a free and independent nation the lawmakers in various commonwealths soon addressed themselves to the task of enacting protective measures for insuring the continuance of the supply of desirable game birds and animals. But as the years went by, and the game showed every indication of continuing to decrease despite the measures that had been adopted for their benefit, other and more stringent game laws were enacted.

In the fullness of time there came into being in every state in the Union an extensive, complex system of prohibitive measures regarding seasons for hunting, methods of killing, size of bag limit, restrictions on sale, and limiting the kinds of game that might be killed.

Many states also went into the business of rearing, in a condition of semi-captivity. Pheasants, grouse, Hungarian Partridges, Quail, Ducks, and some other species of birds highly esteemed as food, the object of this being to restock covers that had been depleted of bird-life by excessive shooting, or to supply new attraction for field-sports in regions where other game was limited.

Theoretically the methods adopted by the several states were sure to keep the numbers of game birds up to a point where a reasonable amount of sport might be engaged in by those of our citizens who enjoy the excitement and recreation of going afield with gun and dog. It could easily be proven on paper that by judiciously regulating the shooting, {176} and having this conform to the available game supply, every state could at one and the same time preserve the different species, and furnish satisfactory shooting for its sportsmen.

But in practice the theory failed to work as expected; the gunners were on hand every fall in increasing numbers but the birds continued to grow scarcer.

In the vernacular of the sportsman, birds that may legitimately be shot are divided for convenience into three groups, viz., upland game birds, water fowl, and shore birds. It is in reference to the fortunes of the water fowl and shore birds that the greatest apprehension has been felt. Approximately all of the species concerned are of migratory habits. The open seasons when these may be hunted vary greatly in different states and all attempts to get anything like uniform laws in the various hunting territories have been attended with failure.

It became clear in time that the most important action that could be taken to conserve these birds {177} was to prohibit shooting during the spring migration, when the birds were on their way to their northern breeding grounds. Some states adopted this measure and the results bore out the predictions of those who urged the passage of such laws. New York State, for example, tried the experiment, and within two years thousands of Black Ducks were breeding where for a long time they had not been known to occur in summer. So the feeling became general among bird protectors that it would be an excellent thing if spring shooting of all migratory game birds should be stopped everywhere. But the legislatures of many states paid small heed to the little minority of their constituents who voiced such sentiments, and the problem of how to bring about the desired results remained unsolved.

[Illustration: Egret brooding on a Florida island owned and guarded by the Audubon Society.]

The Theory of Shiras.--In the year 1904 a United States Congressman announced to the country that he had found the proper solution for settling once and for all the question of spring shooting, and for putting to an end the ceaseless wrangling that {178} continually went on in the various legislatures when the subject was brought up. This gentleman, George Shiras, 3rd, planned to cut the Gordian knot by turning over to the Federal Government the entire subject of making laws regarding the killing of migratory game birds.

In December that year he introduced a bill in Congress covering his ideas on the subject. This radical proposition created merriment in certain legal circles. Was it not written in the statutes of nearly every state that the birds and game belong to the people of the state? Therefore what had the Government to do with the subject? Furthermore, were there not numerous court decisions upholding the authority of the states in their declarations of ownership of the birds and game? Others saw in this move only another attempt toward increasing the power of the central government, and depriving the states further of their inalienable rights. This remarkable document was discussed to some extent but nothing was done. Four years later {179} Congressman John W. Weeks reintroduced the bill with slight modifications. Nothing came of this any more than of the bill that he started going in 1909. In 1911 he again brought forward this pet measure toward which Congress had so often turned a cold shoulder. Senator George P. McLean set a similar bill afloat in the troubled waters of the Senate. Nothing happened, however, until the spring of 1912, when committee hearings were given on these bills in both branches of Congress. Representatives of more than thirty organizations interested in conservation appeared and eloquently sought to impress the national lawmakers with the importance and desirability of the measure. Both bills were intended for the protection of migratory game birds only, but the representative of the National Association of Audubon Societies urged that the bills be extended to include all migratory insect-eating birds, because of their value to agriculture. This suggestion was adopted and after a stiff fight in Congress the McLean Bill became a law on March 4, 1913.

This new federal statute did not in itself change any of the existing game laws, but it gave authority to certain functionaries to make such regulations as they deemed wise, necessary, and proper to extend better protection to all migratory game and insect-eating birds in the United States. The Secretary of Agriculture, to whose department this unusual duty was assigned, read the law thoughtfully, concluded that the task did not come within the bounds of his personal capabilities, and very wisely turned the whole matter over to a committee of three experts chosen from one of the department bureaus and known as the Biological Survey.

The Work of the Committee.--This committee at once began the preparation of a series of regulations to give effect to the new statute. Drawing extensively from the records stored in the Survey offices, and seasoning these with their own good judgment and knowledge of existing conditions, they brought out in a period of three months and nine days, or to be more precise, on June 23, 1913, a set of ten {181} regulations which, in many ways, have revolutionized shooting in the United States.

These were printed in pamphlet form and distributed widely; for before they could have the effect of laws it was necessary that they should be advertised for a period of at least three months in order to give all dissatisfied parties an opportunity to be heard.

The whole idea of the Government taking over the matter of protecting migratory birds, as well as the startling character of some of the regulations promulgated by the committee was justly expected to bring forth either great shouts of approbation or a storm of disapproval, and possibly both sounds might be heard. As long experience has shown that it is necessary to have public opinion approve of a game law if it is to be effective, one can well understand that, following the mailing of the circular of rules, these gentlemen of the committee stood with hand to brow and anxiously scanned the distant horizon. Nor did they have long to wait before {182} critical rumblings began to be heard in many directions, for it is always hard for men to give up privileges which they have once enjoyed.

In fact, as the committee waited, the sky began rapidly to fill with interrogation points; for it has ever been the case that the dissatisfied ones of earth are louder in their objections than are the satisfied ones in their commendations.

As a matter of fact, the regulations on the whole were remarkable for their clearness, directness, and fairness. They came nearer being formed for the benefit of the birds instead of for the pleasure and convenience of the hunters, than any general far-reaching bird-protective measure, which has been enacted in this country.

For the purpose of the regulations, migratory game birds were defined as Ducks, Geese, Swans, Rails, Coots, Pigeons, Cranes, and shore birds, which included Plover, Snipe, Woodcock, and Sandpipers. Migratory insectivorous birds were enumerated as Thrushes, Orioles, Larks, Swallows, Wrens, {183} Woodpeckers, and all other perching birds that feed entirely or chiefly on insects.

Having thus conveniently classified migratory birds into two easily comprehensible and distinguishable groups, the way was open to deal with them separately and distinctively. Therefore, after declaring it to be illegal to kill any bird of either class between sunset and sunrise, the regulations went on to state that insect-eating birds shall not be killed in any place or in any manner, even in the daytime.

Among other things this provision, by one stroke, completed the campaign which the Audubon Society had been waging for long years on behalf of the Robin. In Maryland, North Carolina, Mississippi, Louisiana and Tennessee, the Robin-potpie-loving inhabitants must in future content themselves with such game birds as Quail, Grouse, Wild Turkeys, and Ducks. The life of Sir Robin Redbreast has now been declared to be sacred everywhere. He and his mate are to dwell beneath the protection of the strong arm of the United States Government.

{184} Another feature of the Audubon work was also completed by this section of the new regulations. This is the safeguarding of all song and insect-eating birds in the States of Montana, Idaho, Nevada, Utah, Arizona, Nebraska, Kansas, and New Mexico, constituting the group of states whose legislatures had thus far withstood the importunities of the Audubon workers to extend protection to such birds.

Regulation Number Four provided for an absolute closed hunting season on sixty-two species of water birds until September, 1918.

The above includes what we might call some of the minor regulations proposed by the Biological Survey Committee. Then comes the big regulation, the one which was of absorbing interest to every member of the vast army of five million hunters in the United States. This is the regulation which divides the country into zones and prescribes the shooting seasons in each. Touching on this point the Government experts already mentioned gave out this statement by way of explanation:

Government Explanations.--"More than fifty separate seasons for migratory birds were provided under statutes in force in 1912. This multiplicity of regulations of zones to suit special localities has apparently had anything but a beneficial effect on the abundance of game. The effort to provide special seasons for each kind of game in each locality merely makes a chain of open seasons for migratory birds and allows the continued destruction of such birds from the beginning of the first season to the close of the last. It is believed that better results will follow the adoption of the fewest possible number of zones and so regulating the seasons in each as to include the time when such species is in the best condition or at the maximum of abundance during the autumn. For this reason the country has been divided into two zones, as nearly equal as possible, one to include the states in which migratory game birds breed, or would breed if given reasonable protection, the other the states in which comparatively few species breed, but in which many winter. {186} Within these zones the seasons are fixed for the principal natural groups, water fowl, Rails, shore birds, and Woodcock. In no case does the zone boundary cross a state line, and except in very rare cases the seasons are uniform throughout the states."

With few changes the regulations were finally adopted. Wherever the federal law conflicted with a state law, the former was regarded as supreme, and to make things more generally uniform the states have since been changing their laws to conform to the Government regulations. After being tried out for three years these rules recently were modified by making five shooting zones and altering certain other provisions. These last regulations which became effective on August 21, 1916, to-day stand as the law of the land affecting migratory birds.

To the United States Biological Survey was intrusted the task of enforcing the law by means of game wardens and other officials. That is, the survey was to collect the evidence in cases of violations, and the prosecutions were to be conducted {187} by the Department of Justice. To enable these officials to execute the law, Congress has appropriated $50,000 annually--which is just about one tenth the minimum amount needed for the purpose. This paltry sum has been expended as judiciously as possible with marked results for good. Trouble, however, soon developed in the courts. One autumn day Harvey C. Schauver went a-hunting on Big Lake, Arkansas, and finding no Ducks handy he shot a Coot, which was against the law. When the case came up in the Federal Court of Eastern Arkansas, the judge who presided declared that the federal law under which the defendant was being tried was unconstitutional, and wrote a lengthy decision, giving his reasons for holding this view. Within the next two months two other federal courts rendered similar decisions.

At this point the Department of Justice decided to bring no further cases to trial until the United States Supreme Court should pass on the constitutionality of the law, the Arkansas case having {188} already been brought before this tribunal. At this writing the decision has not been rendered.

Only Bird Treaty in the World.--Early in the history of the operations of this law the possibilities of an adverse decision by the Supreme Court were considered by those interested in the measure, and a plan was found whereby all might not be lost if such a catastrophe should occur. The first movement in this new direction was made by Elihu Root on January 14, 1913, when he introduced in the Senate a resolution requesting the President to propose to the other governments the negotiation of a convention for the protection of birds. A proposed bird treaty between this country and Canada was then drawn up, and after much effort was brought to a successful issue and was finally ratified by Congress on September 29, 1916.

This treaty broadly covers the provisions of the Migratory Bird Law in this country, so if the Supreme Court declares the latter to be invalid the Government still stands committed to the {189} principals of migratory bird-protection by virtue of the treaty.

So the long fight to stop spring shooting and provide short uniform closed seasons for shooting shore birds and wild fowl is drawing to a glorious conclusion.

To-day, in the history of wild-life conservation, we have before us the unusual spectacle of the United States Government taking a serious hand in a problem which had been found to be too difficult of solution by the different states working separately. Many of us believe this predicts a brighter day for the perpetuation of the wild life of our country.

CHAPTER X

BIRD RESERVATIONS

The creation of reservations where wild birds can be protected at all times is a modern idea, brought prominently to public attention by the efforts of the Audubon Society. The first interest that the United States Government manifested in the subject was about thirteen years ago. On May 29, 1901, the legislature of Florida was induced to enact a statute making it a misdemeanour to kill any non-game birds of the State with the exception of the Crow and a few other species regarded by the lawmakers as being injurious to man's interests.

First Federal Bird Reservation--Shortly afterward the Audubon Society friends employed a man to protect from the raids of tourists and feather hunters a {191} large colony of Brown Pelicans that used for nesting purposes a small, muddy, mangrove-covered island in Indian River on the Atlantic Coast. Soon murmurings began to be heard. "Pelicans eat fish and should not be protected," declared one Floridan. "We need Pelican quills to sell to the feather dealers," chimed in another with a keen eye to the main chance. There was talk of repealing the law at the next session of the legislature, and the hearts of the Audubon workers were troubled. At first they thought of buying the island, so as to be in a position to protect its feathered inhabitants by preventing trespass. However, it proved to be unsurveyed Government land, and the idea was suggested of getting the Government to make a reservation for the protection of the birds. The matter was submitted to President Roosevelt, who no sooner ascertained the facts that the land was not suited for agricultural purposes, and that the Audubon Society would guard it, than with characteristic directness he issued the following remarkable edict: "It is hereby ordered that Pelican {192} Island in Indian River is reserved and set apart for the use of the Department of Agriculture as a preserve and breeding ground for native birds."

The gist of this order, bearing the authorization of the Secretary of Agriculture, was quickly painted on a large sign, and placed on the island, where all who sailed near might read. Imagine the chagrin of the Audubon workers upon learning from their warden that when the Pelicans returned that season to occupy the island as before, they took one look at this declaration of the President and immediately departed, one and all, to a neighbouring island entirely outside of the reservation! Signs less alarming in size were substituted, and the Pelicans, their feelings appeased, condescended to return, and have since dwelt peacefully under the protecting care of the Government.

Congressional Sanction.--In view of the fact that some persons contended that the President had over-stepped his authority in making a bird reservation, a law was drafted, and passed by Congress, specifically {193} giving protection to birds on lands set apart as National bird reservations. The legal difficulties thus removed, the way lay open for the creation of other bird reservations, and the Audubon Society seized the opportunity. Explorations were started to locate other Government territories containing important colonies of water birds. This work was quickly extended over many parts of the United States. Hunters of eggs and plumes were busy plying their trades wherever birds were known to assemble in great numbers, and the work had to be hurried if the birds were to be saved.

Mr. Frank M. Miller, of New Orleans, reported a case in which five thousand eggs had been broken on one Louisiana island inhabited by sea birds in order that fresh eggs might subsequently be gathered into the boats waiting at anchor off shore. No wonder that friends of water birds were profoundly concerned about their future welfare, and hailed with delight Mr. Roosevelt's quick action.

Mr. William Dutcher, President of the National {194} Association of Audubon Societies, was so much pleased with the results achieved by the Federal reservation work of 1905, that he declared in his annual report that the existence of the Association was justified if it had done nothing more than secure Federal bird reservations and had helped to guard them during the breeding season.

That year President Roosevelt established four more bird refuges. One of these, Stump Lake, in North Dakota, became an important nursery for Gulls, Terns, Ducks, and Cormorants in summer, and a safe harbour for wild fowl during the spring and fall migrations. Huron Island and Siskiwit in Lake Superior, the homes of innumerable Herring Gulls, were made perpetual bird sanctuaries, and Audubon wardens took up their lonely watch to guard them against all comers.

Florida Reservations.--At the mouth of Tampa Bay, Florida, is a ninety-acre island, Passage Key. Here the wild bird life of the Gulf Coast has swarmed in the mating season since white man first knew the {195} country. Thousands of Herons of various species, as well as Terns and shore birds, make this their home. Dainty little Ground Doves flutter in and out among the cactus on the sheltered sides of the sand dunes; Plovers and Sandpipers chase each other along the beaches, and the Burrowing Owls here hide in their holes by night and roam over the island by day.

When this place was described to President Roosevelt, he immediately declared that the birds must not be killed there without the consent of the Secretary of Agriculture. With one stroke of his pen he brought this desirable condition into existence, and Mrs. Asa Pillsbury was duly appointed to protect the island. She is one of the few women bird wardens in America.

These things happened in the early days of Government work for the protection of water birds. The Audubon Society had found a new field for endeavour, highly prolific in results. With the limited means at its command the work of ornithological exploration was carried forward. Every island, mud flat, and sand bar along the coast of the Mexican {196} Gulf, from Texas to Key West, was visited by trained ornithologists who reported their findings to the New York office. These were forwarded to Washington for the approval of Dr. T. S. Palmer of the Biological Survey, and Frank Bond, of the General Land Office, where executive orders were prepared for the President's signature.

The Breton Island Reservation off the coast of Louisiana, including scores of islands and bars, was established in 1904. Six additional reservations were soon created along the west coast of Florida, thus extending a perpetual guardianship over the colonies of sea and coastwise birds in that territory-- the pitiful remnants of vast rookeries despoiled to add to the profits of the millinery trade.

The work was early started in the West resulting in the Malheur Lake and Klamath Lake reservations of Oregon. The latter is to-day the summer home of myriads of Ducks, Geese, Grebes, White Pelicans, and other wild waterfowl, and never a week passes that the waters of the lake are not fretted with the {197} prow of the Audubon patrol boat, as the watchful warden extends his vigil over the feathered wards of our Government.

Federal bird reservations have been formed not only of lakes with reedy margins and lonely islands in the sea, they have been made to include numerous Government reservoirs built in the arid regions of the West.

Distant Reservations.--Once set in motion, this movement for Federal bird reservations soon swept beyond the boundaries of the United States. One was established in Porto Rico, and several others among the islands of Alaska, on whose rocky cliffs may be seen to-day clouds of Puffins, Auks, and Guillemots--queer creatures that stand upright like a man--crowding and shouldering each other about on the ledges which overlook the dark waters of Bering Sea. One reservation in Alaska covers much of the lower delta of the Yukon, including the great tundra country south of the river, embracing within its borders a territory greater than the {198} State of Connecticut. From the standpoint of preserving rare species of birds this is doubtless one of the most important reservations which has come into existence. It is here that many of the wild fowl, which frequent the California coast in winter, find a summer refuge safe alike from the bullet of the white man and the arrow of the Indian. Here it is that the lordly Emperor Goose is probably making his last stand on the American continent against the aggressions of the destructive white race.

Away out in the western group of the Hawaiian Archipelago are located some of the world's most famous colonies of birds. From remote regions of the Pacific sea birds journey hither when the instinct for mating is strong upon them. Here come "Love Birds" or White Terns, and Albatrosses, great winged wonders whose home is on the rolling deep. The number seems almost beyond belief to men and women unfamiliar with bird life in congested colonies. On February 3, 1909, these islands and reefs were included in an executive order whereby {199} the "Hawaiian Island Reservation" was brought into existence. This is the largest of all our Government bird reserves. It extends through more than five degrees of longitude.

At intervals in the past these islands had been visited by vessels engaged in the feather trade, and although no funds were available for establishing a warden patrol among them, it was fondly hoped that the notice to the world that these birds were now wards of the United States would be sufficient to insure their safety.

A rude shock was felt, therefore, when late that year a rumour reached Washington that a Japanese poaching vessel had been sighted heading for these waters. The revenue cutter Thetis, then lying at Honolulu, was at once ordered on a cruise to the bird islands. Early in 1910 the vessel returned, bringing with her twenty-three Japanese feather hunters who had been captured at their work of destruction. In the hold of the vessel were stored two hundred and fifty-nine thousand pairs of wings, {200} two and a half tons of baled feathers, and several large cases and boxes of stuffed birds. Had the Japanese escaped with their booty they would have realized over one hundred thousand dollars for their plunder. This island was again raided by feather collectors in the spring of 1915.

President Taft a Bird Protectionist.--President Taft continued the policy of creating bird reservations begun by Mr. Roosevelt, and a number were established during his administration. President Wilson likewise is a warm advocate of bird protection. One of many reservations he has created is the Panama Canal Zone, which is in charge of the Panama Canal Commission. With this exception and that of the Pribilof Reservation, which is in charge of the Bureau of Fisheries, all Government bird reservations are under the care of the Department of Agriculture, and their administration is directed by the Bureau of the Biological Survey. The National Association of Audubon Societies still contributes in a modest way to the financial support of some of the wardens. {201} Below is given a full list of the Federal bird reservations created up to January, 1917, with the dates, and in the order of, their establishment:

LIST OF NATIONAL BIRD RESERVATIONS

NO. NAME DATE OF ESTABLISHMENT

1. Pelican Island, Fla. . . . . Mar. 14, 1903 2. Breton Island, La. . . . . Oct. 4, 1904 3. Stump Lake, N. Dak. . . . . Mar. 9, 1905 4. Huron Islands, Mich. . . . . Oct. 10, 1905 5. Siskiwit Islands, Mich. . . . . Oct. 10, 1905 6. Passage Key, Fla. . . . . Oct. 10, 1905 7. Indian Key, Fla. . . . . Feb. 10, 1906 8. Tern Islands, La. . . . . Aug. 8, 1907 9. Shell Keys, La. . . . . Aug. 17, 1907 10. Three Arch Rocks, Oregon . . . . Oct. 14, 1907 11. Flattery Rocks, Wash. . . . . Oct.

23, 1907 12. Quillayute Needles, Wash. . . . . Oct. 23, 1907 13. Copalis Rock, Wash. . . . . Oct. 23, 1907 14. East Timbalier, La. . . . . Dec. 7, 1907 15. Mosquito Inlet, Fla. . . . . Feb. 24, 1908 16. Tortugas Keys, Fla. . . . . Apr. 6, 1908 17. Key West, Fla. . . . . Aug. 8, 1908 18. Klamath Lake, Oregon . . . . Aug. 8, 1908 19. Lake Malheur, Oregon . . . . Aug. 18, 1908 20. Chase Lake, N. Dak. . . . . Aug. 28, 1908 21. Pine Island, Fla. . . . . Sept. 15, 1908 22. Palma Sola, Fla. . . . . Sept. 26, 1908 23. Matlacha Pass, Fla. . . . . Sept. 26, 1908 24. Island Bay, Fla. . . . . Oct. 23, 1908 25. Lock-Katrine, Wyo. . . . . Oct. 26, 1908 26. Hawaiian Islands, Hawaii. . . . . Feb. 3, 1909 27. Salt River, Ariz. . . . . Feb. 25, 1909 28. East Park, Cal. . . . . Feb. 25, 1909 {202}

29. Deer Flat, Idaho . . . . Feb. 25, 1909 30. Willow Creek, Mont. . . . . Feb. 25, 1909 31. Carlsbad, N. Mex. . . . . Feb. 25, 1909 32. Rio Grande, N. Mex. . . . . Feb. 25, 1909 33. Cold Springs, Oregon . . . . Feb. 25, 1909 34. Belle Fourche, S. Dak. . . . . Feb. 25, 1909 35. Strawberry Valley, Utah . . . . Feb. 25, 1909 36. Keechelus, Wash. . . . . Feb. 25, 1909 37. Kachess, Wash. . . . . Feb. 25, 1909 38. Clealum, Wash. . . . . Feb. 25, 1909 39. Bumping Lake, Wash. . . . . Feb. 25, 1909 40. Conconully, Wash. . . . . Feb. 25, 1909 41. Pathfinder, Wyo. . . . . Feb. 25, 1909 42. Shoshone, Wyo. . . . . Feb. 25, 1909 43. Minidoka, Idaho . . . . Feb. 25, 1909 44. Bering Sea, Alaska . . . . Feb. 27, 1909 45. Tuxedni, Alaska . . . . Feb. 27, 1909 46. St. Lazaria, Alaska . . . . Feb. 27, 1909 47. Yukon Delta, Alaska . . . . Feb. 27, 1909 48. Culebra, P. R. . . . . Feb. 27, 1909 49. Farallon, Calif. . . . . Feb. 27, 1909 50. Pribilof, Alaska . . . . Feb. 27, 1909 51. Bogoslof, Alaska . . . . Mar. 2, 1909 52. Clear Lake, Calif. . . . . Apr. 11, 1911 53. Forrester Island, Alaska . . . . Jan. 11, 1913 54. Hazy Islands, Alaska . . . . Jan. 11, 1913 55. Niobrara, Nebr. . . . . Jan. 11, 1913 56. Green Bay, Wis. . . . . Feb. 21, 1913 57. Chamisso Island, Alaska . . . . Dec. 7, 1912 58. Pishkun, Montana. . . . . Dec. 17, 1912 59. Desecheo Island, P. R. . . . . Dec. 19, 1912 60. Gravel Island, Wis. . . . . Jan. 9, 1913 61. Aleutian Islands, Alaska . . . . Mar. 3, 1913 62. Walker Lake, Ark. . . . . Apr. 31, 1913

63. Petit Bois Island, Ala. and Miss. . . . . . . May 6, 1913 64. Anaho Island, Nevada. . . . . Sept. 4, 1913 65. Smith Island, Wash. . . . . June 6, 1914 66. Ediz Hook, Wash. . . . . Jan. 20, 1915 67. Dungeness Spit, Wash. . . . . Jan. 20, 1915 68. Big Lake, Arkansas . . . . Aug. 2, 1915 69. Goat Island, California . . . . Aug. 9, 1916 70. North Platte, Nebraska . . . . Aug. 21, 1916

Audubon Society Reservations.--It may be noted from this list that there are no Government bird reservations in the original thirteen colonies. The reason is that there are no Government waste lands containing bird colonies in these states. To protect the colony-breeding birds found there other means were necessary. The Audubon Society employs annually about sixty agents to guard in summer the more important groups of water birds along the Atlantic Coast and about some of the lakes of the interior. Water-bird colonies are usually situated on islands where the birds are comparatively free from the attacks of natural enemies; hence the question of guarding them resolves itself mainly into the question of keeping people from disturbing the birds {204} during the late spring and summer months. Painted signs will not do this. Men hired for the purpose constitute the only adequate means. Some of the protected islands have been bought or leased by the Audubon Society, but in many cases they are still under private ownership and the privilege of placing a guard had to be obtained as a favour from the owner. Probably half a million breeding water birds now find protection in the Audubon reservations. On the islands off the Maine coast the principal birds safeguarded by this means are the Herring Gull, Arctic Tern, Wilson's Tern, Leach's Petrel, Black Guillemot, and Puffin. There are protected colonies of Terns on Long Island; of Terns and Laughing Gulls on the New Jersey coast; of Black Skimmers, and of various Terns, in Virginia and North Carolina.

One of the greatest struggles the Audubon Society has ever had has been to raise funds every year for the protection of the colonies of Egrets and Ibis in the South Atlantic States. The story of this fight is longer than {205} can be told in one short chapter. The protected colonies are located mainly in the low swampy regions of North Carolina, South Carolina, Georgia, and Florida. I have been in many of these "rookeries" and know that the warden who undertakes to guard one of them takes his life in his hand. Perhaps a description of one will answer more or less for the twenty other Heron colonies the Society has under its care.

The Corkscrew Rookery.--Some time ago I visited the warden of this reservation, located in the edge of the "Big Cypress" Swamp thirty-two miles south of Ft. Myers, Florida. Arriving at the colony late in the evening, after having travelled thirty miles without seeing a human being or a human habitation, we killed a rattlesnake and proceeded to make camp. The shouting of a pair of Sandhill Cranes awakened us at daylight, and, to quote Greene, the warden, the sun was about "two hands high" when we started into the rookery. We crossed a glade two hundred yards wide and then entered the swamp. Progress {206} was slow, for the footing was uncertain and the tall sawgrass cut our wrists and faces.

There are many things unspeakably stimulating about a journey in such a tropical swamp. You work your way through thick, tangled growths of water plants and hanging vines. You clamber over huge fallen logs damp with rank vegetation, and wade through a maze of cypress "knees." Unwittingly, you are sure to gather on your clothing a colony of ravenous ticks from some swaying branch. Redbugs bent on mischief scramble up on you by the score and bury themselves in your skin, while a cloud of mosquitoes waves behind you like a veil. In the sombre shadows through which you move you have a feeling that there are many unseen things that crawl and glide and fly, and a creepy feeling about the edges of your scalp becomes a familiar sensation. Once we came upon the trail of a bear and found the going easier when we waded on hands and knees through the opening its body had made.

In the more open places the water was completely {207} covered with floating plants that Greene called "wild lettuce." These appeared to be uniform in size, and presented an absolutely level surface except in a few places where slight elevations indicated the presence of inquisitive alligators, whose gray eyes we knew were watching our movements through the lettuce leaves.

Although the swamp was unpleasant under foot, we had but to raise our eyes to behold a world of beauty. The purple blossoms of air plants, and the delicate petals of other orchids greeted us everywhere. From the boughs overhead long streamers of gray Spanish moss waved and beckoned in the breeze. Still higher, on gaunt branches of giant cypresses a hundred feet above our heads, great, grotesque Wood Ibises were standing on their nests, or taking flight for their feeding grounds a dozen miles southward.

We were now fairly in the midst of an immense bird city, and some of the inhabitants were veritable giants in the bird world. The body of a Wood Ibis {209} is about the size of a Turkey hen. Its long, bare neck terminates in a most remarkable fashion, for the top of the head is not only innocent of feathers but also destitute of skin--"Flintheads," the people call the bird. Its bill is nearly ten inches long, slightly curved and very massive. Woe to the unlucky fish or luckless rat upon whom a blow falls from the Flinthead's heavy beak! There were probably one hundred thousand of these birds inhabiting Corkscrew Rookery at the time of my visit. There were also large colonies of the smaller White Ibis and several varieties of Heron. Eight of the almost extinct Roseate Spoonbills wheeled into view above the swamp, but quickly passed from sight.

The most interesting birds, those concerning which the Audubon Society is most solicitous, are the White Egrets. These snow-white models of grace and beauty have been persecuted for their plumes almost to the point of extermination, and here is situated the largest assemblage of them left in Florida.

"Those 'long whites' are never off my mind for a {210} minute," said the warden, as we paused to watch some fly over. "Two men came to my camp last week who thought I didn't know them, but I did. They were old-time plume hunters. They said they were hunting cattle, but I knew better--they were after Egrets and came to see if I was on guard. I told them if they saw any one after plumes to pass {211} the word that I would shoot on sight any man with a gun who attempted to enter the Corkscrew. I would do it, too," he added as he tapped the barrel of his Winchester. "It is terrible to hear the young birds calling for food after the old ones have been killed to get the feathers for rich women to wear. I am not going to have my birds sacrificed that way."

The teeming thousands of birds in this rookery feed their young to a more or less extent on fish, and from the nests many fragments fall into the mud and water below. In the wise economy of nature few objects of real value are suffered to go to waste. Resting on the water plants, coiled on logs, or festooned in the low bushes, numerous cotton-mouthed water-moccasins lie in wait. Silently and motionless they watch and listen, now and then raising their heads when a light splash tells them of the approach of some heedless frog, or of the falling of some dead fish like manna from the nests above. May is the dry season, and the low water of the swamp accounted in a measure for the unusual number of snakes to {212} be seen. Exercising a fair amount of caution, I slew that morning fourteen poisonous reptiles, one of which measured more than five feet in length and had a girth I was just able to encompass with both hands.

Wardens Shot by Plume Hunters.--This is a region where the Audubon warden must constantly keep his lonely watch, for should he leave even for a short time there would be danger of the colony being raided and the protective work of many seasons wiped out. A successful shooting trip of plume hunters to the Corkscrew might well net the gunners as much as five thousand dollars, and in a country where money is scarce that would mean a magnificent fortune. The warden is fully alive to this fact, and is ever on the alert. Many of the plume hunters are desperate men, and he never knows what moment he may need to grasp his rifle to defend his life in the shadows of the Big Cypress, where alligators and vultures would make short shrift of his remains.

He remembers, as he goes his rounds among the birds day by day, or lies in his tent at night, that a {213} little way to the south, on a lonely sand key, lies buried Guy Bradley, who was done to death by plume hunters while guarding for the Audubon Society the Cuthbert Egret Rookery. On Orange Lake, northward, the warden in charge still carries in his body a bullet from a plume gatherer's gun. Only three days before my visit Greene's nearest brother warden on duty at the Alligator Bay Colony had a desperate rifle battle with four poachers who, in defiance of law and decency, attempted to shoot the Egrets which he was paid to protect.

I like to think of Greene as I saw him the last night in camp, his brown, lean face aglow with interest as he told me many things about the birds he guarded. The next day I was to leave him, and night after night he would sit by his fire, a lonely representative of the Audubon Society away down there on the edge of the Big Cypress, standing as best he could between the lives of the birds he loved and the insatiable greed of Fashion.

CHAPTER XI

MAKING BIRD SANCTUARIES

The best place to study wild birds is on a reservation, for there birds have greatly lost their fear of man, and primitive conditions have been largely restored. In one of the southern sea-bird colonies I have photographed Royal Terns standing unafraid on the sands not twelve feet distant. They had become so accustomed to the warden in charge that they had regained their confidence in man. At Lake Worth I saw a gentleman feed Scaup Ducks that swam to within two yards of his boat. In thousands of dooryards throughout the country wild birds, won by kind treatment, now take their food or drink within a few feet of their human protectors. The dooryards have become little bird reservations. I have several {215} friends who regularly feed Chickadees in winter, perched on their outstretched hands. It is astonishing how quickly wild creatures respond to a reasonable treatment. This may readily be learned by any householder who will try the experiment. With a little patience any teacher can instruct her pupils in the simple art of making the birds feel at home in the vicinity of the schoolhouse.

Natural Nesting Places Destroyed.--Some kinds of birds, as far back as we know their history, have built their nests in the holes of trees. Woodpeckers have strong, chisel-shaped bills and are able to excavate nesting cavities, but there are others that do not possess such tools. These must depend on finding the abandoned hole of some Woodpecker, or the natural hollow of some tree. It not infrequently happens that such birds are obliged to search far and wide for a hole in which they can make their abode. It is customary for those who take care of lawns and city parks to chop away and remove all dead limbs or dead trees. As very few Woodpeckers ever attempt {217} to dig a nesting hole in a living tree, such work of the axeman means that when the season comes for the rearing of young, all mated Woodpeckers must move on to where more natural conditions await them. This results in an abnormal reduction of the number of holes for the use of the weaker-billed hole-nesting species, and they must seek the few available hollows or knot-holes. Even these places are often taken away from them, for along comes the tree doctor, who, in his purpose of aiding to preserve the trees, fills up the natural openings with cement and the birds are literally left out in the cold. It is plainly to be seen, therefore, that one reason why more birds do not remain in our towns through the spring months is the absence of places where they can lay their eggs and rear their young.

Nesting Boxes for Birds.--To overcome this difficulty the Audubon Society several years ago began to advocate the erection of suitable nesting boxes, and to-day the practice is gaining wide usage. More persons every year are putting such boxes upon poles {218} or nailing them to trees about their homes, and some city authorities include bird boxes in the annual expenditure for the care of public parks. It was not much more than a decade ago that the first serious commercial attempt was made to place bird boxes on the market. To-day there are not less than twenty firms engaged in their manufacture. Some of the boxes are very ornate and make beautiful additions even to the most carefully kept estate. One can buy them at prices varying from thirty-five cents to thirty-five dollars each. Among the many responsible manufacturers that may be recommended are:

The Crescent Company, "Birdville," Toms River, New Jersey; Pinedale Bird Nesting Box Company, Wareham, Massachusetts; The Audubon Bird House Company, Meriden, New Hampshire; Maplewood Biologica Laboratory, Stamford, Connecticut; Jacobs Bird House Company, 404 South Washington St., Waynesburg, Pa.; Decker Brothers, Rhinebeck, New York; Winthrop Packard, Canton, Massachusetts.

It is not necessary, however, to buy boxes to put {220} up for birds. Equally useful ones can be made in the Manual Training Department of any school, or in the basement or woodshed at home. If you do not know how to begin, you should buy one bird box and construct others similar for yourself. Men sometimes make the mistake of thinking it is absolutely necessary that such boxes should conform strictly to certain set dimensions. Remember that the cavities in trees and stumps, which birds naturally use, show a wide variety in size, shape, and location. A many-roomed, well-painted Martin house makes a pleasing appearance in the landscape, but may not be attractive to the Martins. As a boy I built up a colony of more than fifteen pairs of these birds by the simple device of rudely partitioning a couple of soap boxes. The entrances to the different rooms were neither uniform in size nor in shape, but were such as an untrained boy could cut out with a hatchet. A dozen gourds, each with a large hole in the side, completed the tenements for this well-contented Martin community.

Some Rules for Making and Erecting Bird Boxes.--Here are a few simple rules on the making and placing of bird boxes:

1. In all nest boxes, except those designed for Martins, the opening should be several inches above the floor, thus conforming to the general plan of a Woodpecker's hole, or natural cavity in a tree.

2. As a rule nest boxes should be erected on poles from ten to thirty feet from the ground, or fastened to the sides of trees where limbs do not interfere with the outlook. The main exception is in the case of Wrens, whose boxes or gourds can be nailed or wired in fruit trees or to the side of buildings.

3. Martin houses should be erected on poles at least twenty feet high, placed well out in the open, not less than one hundred feet from buildings or large trees.

4. All boxes should be taken down after the nesting season and the old nesting material removed.

Size of Bird Boxes.--As to the size of nesting boxes for various species, and the diameter of the entrance hole, I cannot do better than give the dimensions {222} prepared by Ned Dearborn, of the United States Department of Agriculture, Washington, D. C.

DIMENSIONS OF NESTING BOXES

Species Floor Depth Entrance Diameter Height of of above of above cavity cavity floor entrance ground

Inches Inches Inches Inches Feet

Bluebird 5 by 5 8 6 1 1/2 5 to 10 Robin 6 by 8 8 [1] [1] 6 to 15 Chickadee 4 by 4 8 to 10 8 1 1/8 6 to 15 Tufted Titmouse 4 by 4 8 to 10 8 1 1/4 6 to 15 White-breasted Nuthatch 4 by 4 8 to 10 8 1 1/4 12 to 20 House Wren 4 by 4 6 to 8 1 to 6 7/8 6 to 10 Bewick Wren 4 by 4 6 to 8 1 to 6 1 6 to 10 Carolina Wren 4 by 4 6 to 8 1 to 6 1 1/8 6 to 10 Dipper 6 by 6 6 1 3 1 to 3 Violet-green Swallow 5 by 5 6 1 to 6 1 1/2 10 to 15 Tree Swallow 5 by 5 6 1 to 6 1 1/2 10 to 15 Barn Swallow 6 by 6 6 [1] [1] 8 to 12 Martin 6 by 6 6 1 2 1/2 15 to 20 Song Sparrow 6 by 6 6 [2] [2] 1 to 3 House Finch 6 by 6 6 4 2 8 to 12 Phoebe 6 by 6 6 [1] [1] 8 to 12 Crested Flycatcher 6 by 6 8 to 10 8 2 8 to 20 Flicker 7 by 7 16 to 18 16 2 1/2 6 to 20 Red-headed Woodpecker 6 by 6 12 to 15 12 2 12 to 20 Golden-fronted Woodpecker 6 by 6 12 to 15 12 2 12 to 20 Hairy Woodpecker 6 by 6 12 to 15 12 1 1/2 12 to 20 Downy Woodpecker 4 by 4 8 to 10 8 1 1/4 6 to 20 Screech Owl 8 by 8 12 to 15 12 3 10 to 30 Sparrow Hawk 8 by 8 12 to 15 12 3 10 to 30 Saw-whet Owl 6 by 6 10 to 12 10 2 1/2 12 to 20 Barn Owl 10 by 18 15 to 18 4 6 12 to 18 Wood Duck 10 by 18 10 to 15 3 6 4 to 20

[1] One or more sides open.

[2] All sides open.

{223}

The foregoing list does not contain the names of all the kinds of birds which have thus far been induced to occupy these artificial nesting sites, but it has most of them. It should be remembered that hole-nesting birds are the only kind that will ever use a bird box. One need not expect a Meadowlark to leave its nest in the grass for a box on a pole, nor imagine that an Oriole will give up the practice of weaving its swinging cradle on an elm limb to go into a box nailed to the side of the tree.

Feeding Birds.--Much can be done to bring birds about the home or the schoolhouse by placing food where they can readily get it. The majority of land birds that pass the winter in Canada or in the colder parts of the United States feed mainly upon seeds. Cracked corn, wheat, rice, sunflower seed, hemp seed, and bird seed, purchased readily in any town, are, therefore, exceedingly attractive articles of diet. Bread crumbs are enjoyed by many species. Food should not be thrown out on the snow unless there is a crust on it or the snow has been well trampled down. {224} Usually it should be placed on boards. Various feeding plans have been devised to prevent the food from being covered or washed away by snow or rain. Detailed explanations of these can be found in Bulletin No. 1, "Attracting Birds About the Home," issued by the National Association of Audubon Societies. Suet wired to the limb of a tree on the lawn will give comfort and nourishment to many a

Chickadee, Nuthatch and Downy Woodpecker. To make a bird sanctuary nesting sites and food are the first requirements. There appears to be no reason why town and city parks should not be made into places of great attraction for the wild birds.

Community Sanctuaries.--At Meriden, New Hampshire, there is a tract of land containing thirty-two acres of fields and woods, dedicated to the comfort and happiness of wild birds. It is owned by the Meriden Bird Club, and owes its existence largely to the intelligence and enthusiasm of Ernest H. Baynes, bird-lover and lecturer, who lives there. The entire community takes an interest in its maintenance, {225} and there birds are fed and nesting places provided. It is in the widest sense a "community sanctuary." There are now a number of these cooperative bird havens established and cared for in practically the same way. One is in Cincinnati, another in Ithaca, New York, and still another at Greenwich, Connecticut.

Birdcraft Sanctuary.--The best equipped of this class of community bird refuges, as distinguished from private estates, or Audubon Society, State, or Federal bird reservations, is Birdcraft Sanctuary in Fairfield, Connecticut, a tract of ten acres presented to the Connecticut Audubon Society in June, 1914. Mrs. Mabel Osgood Wright, President of the Connecticut Society, has written that in the creation of this sanctuary it was decided that certain requirements were necessary:

"A cat-proof fence to surround the entire place. That it may not look aggressive, it should be set well inside the picturesque old wall. Stone gateposts and a rustic gate at the entrance on the {226} highway. A bungalow for the caretaker, wherein there shall be a room for the meetings of the Society's Executive Committee and Board. A tool and workshop of corresponding style. Several rustic shelters and many seats.

"The assembling of the various springs into a pond, so designed as to make an island of a place where the Redwings nest.

"Trails to be cut through the brush and the turf grass in a charming bit of old orchard on the hilltop, to be restored for the benefit of worm-pulling Robins.

"Several stone basins to be constructed for birdbaths, houses to be put up of all sorts, from Wren boxes, Von Berlepsch model. Flicker and Owl boxes, to a Martin hotel; and, lastly, the supplementing of the natural growth by planting pines, spruces, and hemlocks for windbreaks, and mountain ashes, mulberries, sweet cherries, flowering shrubs and vines for berries and Hummingbird honey."

Not only were all these things done, but there has {227} been built and equipped a small museum of Natural History, unique in its good taste and usefulness.

Cemeteries as Bird Sanctuaries.--The interest in the subject of bird sanctuaries is growing every day; in fact, all America is now planning new homes for her birds--homes where they may live with unrestricted freedom, where food and lodging in abundance, and of the best, will be supplied, where bathing-pools will be at their service, where blossoming trees will welcome them in the spring and fields of grain in the fall, quiet places where these privileges will bring to the birds much joy and contentment. Throughout this country there should be a concerted effort to convert the cemeteries, the homes of our friends who have gone away, into sanctuaries for the bird life of this land. And what isolated spots could be more welcome to the birds than these places that hold so many sad memories for human beings?

No place in the world ought to speak more forcibly to us of the Resurrection than the cemeteries of our land. In them we should hear inspiring bird songs, {228} notice the nesting of birds, and the little ones preparing for their flight into the world. There we should find beautiful flowers and waving grain, typical of that spiritual harvest which should be associated in our minds with comfort and peace.

A Birdless Cemetery.--I visited, not long ago, one of the old-time cemeteries, the pride of a neighbouring city. It was indeed a place of beauty to the eye; but to my mind there is always something flat and insipid about a landscape lacking the music of singing birds. Therefore I looked and listened for my feathered friends. Some English Sparrows flew up from the drive, and I heard the rusty hinge-like notes of a small company of Purple Crackles that were nesting, I suspected, in the pine trees down the slope, but of really cheerful bird life there appeared to be none in this artificially beautified, forty-acre enclosure. There is no reason to suppose that, under normal conditions, birds would shun a cemetery any more than does the traditional graveyard rabbit.

It was not dread of the dead, such as some mortals {229} have, that kept the song birds from this place; it was the work of the living that had driven them away. From one boundary to another there was scarcely a yard of underbrush where a Thrasher or Chewink might lurk, or in which a Redstart, or a dainty Chestnut-sided Warbler, might place its nest. Not a drop of water was discoverable, where a bird might slake its thirst. Neither in limb nor bole was there a single cavity where a Titmouse, Wren, or Bluebird might construct a bed for its young. No fruit-bearing trees were there to invite the birds in summer; nor, so far as I could see, any berry-bearing shrubs such as birds enjoy, nor any weed patches to attract the flocks of Whitethroats and Juncos that come drifting southward with the falling leaves of autumn.

Had my visit to this place been made late in April, or in May, there might have been a different tale to tell. September might also have yielded more birds than June, for September is a season when the migrants are with us for a time. Then the little voyageurs of the upper air are wont to pause after a {230} night of tiresome flight, and rest for the day in any grove that chances to possess even moderate home comforts.

Birds of a New York Graveyard.--Some time ago B. S. Bowdish made a careful study of the bird life of St. Paul's Churchyard, in New York City. This property is three hundred and thirty-three feet long and one hundred and seventy-seven feet wide. In it is a large church and also a church school. Along one side surge the Broadway throngs. From the opposite side come the roar and rumble of an elevated railway. The area contains, according to Mr. Bowdish, three large, ten medium, and forty small trees. With great frequency for two years, field glass in hand, he pursued his work of making a bird census of the graveyard. No bird's nest rewarded his search, for the place was absolutely destitute of feathered songsters during the late spring and summer, and, with a single exception, he never found a bird there in winter. Yet it is interesting to note that in this noisy, limited area, during the {331} periods of migration, he discovered three hundred and twenty-eight birds, embracing forty species.

Why do not more of the birds that pass in spring tarry in this quiet place for the summer? The answer is that the cemetery has been rendered unattractive to them by the merely human committee in charge of the property.

During the season when birds are engaged with their domestic duties they are usually a very wise little people. They know perfectly well whether a region is calculated to provide them with sure and safe nesting sites, and whether sufficient food and water are available for their daily wants. A little of this same wisdom on our part, and a comparatively small expenditure, might make a bird paradise of almost any cemetery. Such places are not usually frequented by men and boys who go afield for the purpose of shooting. That is an important point in the establishment of a bird sanctuary.

Eliminate Enemies.--One great enemy of the birds, however, must be guarded against--the domestic {232} cat. This can be done fairly effectively by means of a cat-proof fence.

Gunners and cats having been eliminated, few other enemies of birds need be seriously considered. Bird-catching Hawks are not often numerous in the neighbourhood of cemeteries. Red squirrels are accused of pilfering from birds' nests, and when abundant they may constitute a menace.

Properly constructed bird boxes, wisely placed, have often proved a means of increasing bird life to an astonishing degree; and they are absolutely the only inducement to hole-nesting varieties to remain during the summer in a cemetery from which all standing dead wood has been removed. Even the strong-billed Woodpecker will not abide in a region where the only trees are living ones, unless, perchance, an artificial nest entices the resplendent and dashing Flicker to tarry. Many a Bluebird, with its azure coat gleaming in the sunlight, visits the cemetery in early spring. From perch to perch he flies, and in his plaintive note can be detected the {233} question that every bird asks of his mate: "Where shall we find a place for our nest?" In the end he flies away. Therefore when the roses and lilies bloom the visitor is deprived of the Bluebird's cheery song, for the little fellow and his mate have departed to the neighbouring farm where they may be found, perhaps, in the old apple orchard.

A few cents expended for lumber and a very little labour in the making of a small box to be attached to the side of a tree or erected on a post, are all that is needed to keep the Bluebirds where they can cheer the hearts of sorrowing visitors. The tiny Wrens, whose loud bursts of song are entirely out of proportion to their size, can be attracted in summer to the proportion of two pairs or more to every acre.

It is a curious fact, of which I believe but little has been written, that birds that build open nests may often be induced to remain in a locality if attractive nesting material is placed within easy reach.

In many a cemetery Orioles could be tempted to weave cradles among the swaying elm limbs if {234} strings and fragments of brightly coloured yarns were placed where the birds could find them. Baron von Berlepsch, whose experiments in attracting birds to his place in Germany have been widely advertised, found that when the tops of bushes were drawn in closely by means of a wire or cord, the resulting thick mass of leaves and twigs offered so fine a place for concealing nests that few birds could resist the temptation to use them.

Other means of rendering a cemetery alluring to nesting birds will readily present themselves when an active interest is developed in the subject. A little thought, a little care, and a little trouble, would make it possible for many birds to dwell in a cemetery, and it must be remembered that unless they can nest there, the chances are that no great volume of bird music will fill the air.

[Illustration: A Bird Bath]

The young of most song birds are fed to a great extent on the soft larvae of insects, of which there is usually an abundant supply everywhere. Many mother birds, however, like to vary this animal diet {235} with a little fruit juice, and the ripened pulp of the blackberry, strawberry, or mulberry, will cheer the spirits of their nestlings. Such fruits in most places are easily grown, and they make a pleasant addition to the birds' menu. In a well-watered territory {236} birds are always more numerous than in a dry region. You may find a hundred of them along the stream in the valley to one on the mountain-top. A cemetery undecorated with fountains, and through or near which no stream flows, is too dry a place for the average bird to risk the exigencies of rearing a family. A few simply constructed fountains or drinking-pools will work wonders in the way of attracting birds to a waterless territory.

In many graveyards considerable unoccupied space might well be planted in buckwheat or some other small grain. If this is left uncut the quantity of nourishing food thus produced will bring together many kinds of grain-eating birds.

Berries and Fruits for Birds.--Many native shrubs and bushes grow berries that birds will come far to gather. Look over the following list which Frederick H. Kennard, of Massachusetts, has recommended, and see if you do not think many of them would be decorative additions to the cemetery. Surely some of them are equal in beauty to many of {237} the shrubs usually planted, and they have the added value of furnishing birds with wholesome food. Here is a part of Mr. Kennard's list: shad-bush, gray, silky, and red osier, cornel, dangleberry, huckleberry, inkberry, black alder, bayberry, shining, smooth, and staghorn sumachs, large-flowering currant, thimbleberry, blackberry, elder, snowberry, dwarf bilberry, blueberry, black haw, hobblebush, and arrow-wood. In the way of fruit-bearing shade trees he recommends sugar maple, flowering dogwood, white and cockspur thorn, native red mulberry, tupelo, black cherry, choke cherry, and mountain ash. For the same purpose he especially recommends the planting of the following vines: Virginia creeper, bull-beaver, frost grape, and fox grape.

Such shrubs and vines are usually well stripped of their berries after the first heavy snowfall. That is the time to begin feeding the birds in earnest. The more food wisely placed where the birds can get it, the more birds you will surely have in the winter. Seeds and grain, with a judicious mixture of animal {238} fat, form the best possible ration for the little feathered pilgrims. Rye, wheat, sunflower seeds, and cracked corn, mixed together in equal parts and accompanied by a liberal sprinkling of ground suet and beef scrap, make an excellent food for birds at this season. This should be placed on shelves attached to trees or buildings, or on oilcloth spread on the snow, or on the ground where the snow has been scraped away. On one occasion the writer attracted many birds by the simple method of providing them with finely pounded fresh beef bones. Furnishing birds with food in winter might well be made a pleasant and profitable duty of the children who attend Sunday-school in rural churches that have graveyards near.

Why should we not make a bird sanctuary of every city park and cemetery in America? Why leave these places to the Sparrows, the Grackles, and perhaps the Starlings, when Bluebirds and Thrushes are within hail, eager to come if the hand of invitation be extended?

CHAPTER XII

TEACHING BIRD STUDY

A little after six o'clock one July morning on the campus of the University of Tennessee, I stood near the centre of a semi-circle of twenty-five school teachers whose expressions indicated a high state of excitement, and whose fifty eyes were riveted on a scene of slaughter but a few feet from them. For five minutes we had scarcely moved. During this time the lives of thirty-two specimens of animal life had been blotted out. The perpetrator of this holocaust was a creature known to scientists as Spizella socialis--called by ordinary people Chipping Sparrow. Its victims were small insects which but a moment before were disporting themselves on the grass.

Preparation of Teachers.--One teacher expressed {240} surprise that a bird could find so many of these choice morsels in so short a time. She had never imagined that so many insects inhabited so small an area as that to which the bird had confined its operations. "Very well," said the instructor, "suppose all of you get down and see how many insects you can find in five minutes." So while he held the watch all proceeded to take part in a bug-hunting contest. In this novel undertaking even the women of the class displayed great zeal. When time was called it was found that one student had a credit of fourteen, another sixteen, a third nineteen, and one tall young woman with glasses exhibited twenty-one insects in the folds of her handkerchief.

A stranger watching the actions of this band of eager, early-rising teachers might have been puzzled to determine what induced them to assemble at this hour of the day for the evident purpose of watching the habits and activities of small birds that the ordinary person passes without notice. They were, nevertheless, occupied in one of the most valuable {241} studies that could have claimed their attention.

[Illustration: Preparing for the coming of the birds. A Junior Audubon class on Prince Edward Island]

For many years the United States Department of Agriculture has been employing trained naturalists to give their time to the investigation of the damage done to growing crops by the insect hosts that infest fields and forests. These and other experts have come forward with astounding statements regarding the destructiveness of birds to insects. We are told, too, that each bird is virtually a living dynamo of energy; that its heart beats twice as fast as the human heart; and that the normal temperature of its blood registers over a hundred degrees. It is a simple fact of biology, therefore, that a tremendous amount of nourishing food is necessary for the bird's existence. Vast quantities of insects are needed for this purpose.

Some time ago a New England gentleman became so impressed by the frequency with which a pair of Robins visited their nest with food for the young that he determined to learn more about the food-consuming {242} possibilities of the four nestlings. The day the offspring left their cradle he temporarily took possession of them. With the aid of some friends, who kindly undertook to dig fishworms for him, he proceeded to give the baby Robins all they cared to eat between daylight and dark. He found to his very great surprise that these small birds consumed in one day food to the amount of their own weight and 56 per cent. additional. If an average-sized man were to eat at this rate he would require seventy pounds of beef and several gallons of water daily. Upon reaching maturity the Robins probably do not eat so greedily, but the incident serves to illustrate their capacity in the days of youth.

The school teachers at the Knoxville Summer School who watched the Chipping Sparrow that morning were members of a group of earnest men and women whose lives were dedicated to the training of children. For nine months they had been in the classroom, meeting heroically the petty trials and annoyances incident to their life work. Now, {243} instead of spending their brief vacation in idleness, they were seeking additional knowledge to prepare them for more valuable future service. They were learning that morning the important lesson that birds are placed on earth for a useful purpose. When they returned to the schoolroom they would teach the boys that the bird is a friend to the farmer and should not be killed nor its nest destroyed. They would teach girls that there is something far more exquisite about the living bird than is to be found in the faded lustre of its feathers when sewed on a hat, and they would cultivate in the heart of the girls a feeling of sympathy for the home life of the birds about them.

The greatest problem to be solved by those actively engaged in measures which make for civic righteousness is how to preserve the children of the country from evil influences, and to direct their curiosity and restless energy into safe and productive channels. The teacher occupies a strategic position in this matter, and one of her problems is how to {244} engage the interest of the child in subjects that are both entertaining and beneficial. Simple lessons in nature study are an excellent method by which to accomplish this end, and a study of out-of-door life should begin with birds.

Bird Study Class.--The systematic instruction of school children in bird study on a careful scientific basis in a large way really had its origin in May, 1910, when Mrs. Russell Sage sent to the National Association of Audubon Societies a cheque for five thousand five hundred dollars with which to inaugurate a plan of bird study in the Southern schools that the writer had outlined to her. She desired that a special effort should be made to arouse interest in the protection of the Robin, which in the Southern States was at that time almost universally regarded as a game bird whose natural destiny was considered to be a potpie. Bird study, it is true, was at that time taught in many city schools, but usually the subject was given slight space in the curriculum, and for the children and {245} teachers there was available only a limited literature, and it was of an inadequate character. A working plan was at once developed whereby literature, coloured pictures of birds, and the Audubon button should be supplied to all the pupils in a school who enrolled themselves as members of an Audubon Class. Each member was required to pay a nominal fee, which, however, was much less than the cost of producing the material received in return.

During the school year that followed the matter was brought to the attention of many of the Southern teachers, and over five hundred Junior Audubon societies resulted, with an enrollment of more than ten thousand children. Following the course of instruction outlined in the literature furnished to the teachers, these children were taught the correct names of many of the common birds, and on field walks they learned to know them by sight. The dates when certain birds were last seen in autumn and first arrived in spring were noted and carefully recorded. Food was given to the birds in winter and {246} bird boxes of various patterns were constructed and placed in parks, orchards, or woods where they would most likely be of service to birds looking for suitable nesting hollows. Bird study was correlated with reading, English composition, history, geography, and even arithmetic.

A Nation-wide Movement.--So successful did this experiment prove that the Audubon workers agreed upon extending this same system into the schools of all the other States in the Union, and the various Provinces of Canada. The fall of 1911, therefore, saw plans well under way for a greatly enlarged scope of work. During the school year, which closed the last of June, 1912, the Association, at a cost of thirteen thousand dollars, enrolled 29,369 school children under the standard bearing the inscription "Protect the Birds."

The movement has continued to grow, and up to June 1, 1916, there had been formed 27,873 classes with a total membership of 559,840 children. The Association is annually expending on this work {247} $25,000 more than the children's fees amount to. Of this amount Mrs. Sage continues to contribute one-fifth, the remaining four-fifths being given by an anonymous friend of children and birds. In supplying these pupils and their teachers with the necessary pictures, leaflets, and outline drawings of birds for colouring, over thirty-one million pages of printed information have been distributed. Pupils have taken hold of this bird study with great zest. Many a dull or inattentive boy, who had been a despair to his teacher and parents, responded to this real nature teaching which took him from his ordinarily uninteresting studies into the wide out of doors. Thousands of teachers have written letters filled with expressions of thankfulness for this opportunity which has come to them and reciting details of the variety of ways in which they have been able to make use of this plan and material for bird study.

What One Teacher Did.--Here, for example, is one from Miss Beth Merritt, who teaches in a little school at Fountain City, Tennessee: "I am very glad to {248} write to you about the Junior Audubon Class we had at school this year. We all enjoyed it exceedingly, and I am sure it did good in the hearts and lives of the little people who were members and in the bird world, too. A year ago I invited the children of some of the other grades to join our Audubon Class and we had over forty members. We had our meetings on Friday afternoons after school. The class was quite successful and we saw some direct results of its success. Several nest-robbing boys gave up that 'sport' altogether. One boy was instrumental in bringing about the arrest of some men who had been shooting song birds. This year I had the class only in my own grade--the second. Almost every child in the room joined, making twenty members. I had daily periods for nature study and language, and every other Friday we used these two periods for the Audubon Class. The children were always anxious for the Audubon Fridays to come. They used often to ask, 'Is tomorrow Bird Day, Miss Beth?' and if I answered in the affirmative, I heard 'Oh, goody,' [248] and 'I won't forget to wear my button,' and 'I wonder what bird it will be,' from every side. Rarely ever did we have an absent mark on Bird Day.

"After we had used all ten of the leaflets you sent us, we had lessons on some of the other birds, or, instead of a regular lesson, we went for a bird walk. I divided the class for these walks, taking ten children at a time. How excited they would get over the birds they saw! Nearly always they could identify the birds themselves, sometimes I helped them, sometimes my bird book helped me, and sometimes we had to write in the notebooks, 'unknown.' I will not try to tell you about all the good results of our Audubon Class that I have noticed. The most important thing I think is that a few more children have a keen interest and a true love for their little brothers of the air. Last year a favourite pastime of a neighbour was shooting birds for his cat, and I think he was no more particular than his cat as to the kind of birds he destroyed. His little daughter was a member of the Audubon Class and this spring I notice our {250} neighbour's cat has to catch its own birds. Perhaps, if the little girl can be an Audubon member another year, there will be no more cat!

"A mother of another little member of the class used to delight in birds' plumes, breasts, or feathers of some kind on her hat. Her spring hat this year was trimmed in ribbon. I have heard several bird lovers say that they have noticed more of our common wild birds about this place than there were last year, and they believe the Junior Audubon societies in the schools have brought about this happy state. When school closed many of the mothers came to me and said that they wished to thank me for what I had done for their children along the line of nature study, especially of birds. They said that they thought the Junior Audubon Class a splendid thing for their children. And

I think it is equally good for the teachers."

Another Junior Club leader, Miss Edna Stafford, a teacher in the public schools of Albany, Indiana, writes: "One day last summer a twelve-year-old boy {251} was out in our street with an airgun shooting at every bird he could see. Recently this same boy came to me with a bird that was hurt, and in a most sympathetic tone said: 'Who do you suppose could have been mean enough to hurt this dear little bird?' Our study of birds in the Junior Audubon Class brought about this change in the boy."

Junior Game Protectors.--Another leader reported from Nashville that the one thousand junior members in the schools there had turned into voluntary bird wardens, and spied upon every man or boy who went afield with a gun. In a number of places the juniors have built and sold bird boxes by hundreds and used the proceeds for advancing the work. In one town the juniors had a most successful tag day, and collected funds that were used to buy grain with which to feed birds in winter. In Connecticut a most helpful and stimulating communication has been established between many of the classes. A junior class in the Logan School, Minneapolis, has even started the publication of a magazine called {252} Owaissa, after the Indian name for Bluebird, as given in Longfellow's "Hiawatha."

Sending Birds' Nests to City Children.--Mrs. Anthony W. Dimock, of Peekamose, New York, makes the following interesting report:

"The Robin Junior Audubon Circle is composed of the boys and girls of three district schools in a Catskill Mountain valley. No one school has enough pupils of required age to form a circle, and the distances between them are so great that frequent meetings cannot be held, but good work is being done.

"The most interesting feature of our work the past year was the collection of abandoned birds' nests in the autumn. One school of five pupils collected over 100 nests. From these collections two selections of ten nests each were made, to be sent to New York City. One collection went to the Jacob Riis Settlement, and one passed through the hands of three kindergartens, interesting 100 children. To each nest was attached a coloured picture of the bird {253} which had made the nest, and a description of its habits. Letters from the Settlement children and the kindergartners brought to the Circle expressions of delightful appreciation."

The National Association of Audubon Societies, with headquarters at 1974 Broadway, New York City, makes the following offer of assistance to those teachers and others who are interested in giving instruction to children on the subject of birds and their usefulness.

To form a Junior Audubon Class for bird study, a teacher should explain to the pupils of her grade (and others if desired) that their object will be to learn all they can about the wild birds, and that every one who becomes a member will be expected to be kind to the birds and protect them. Every member will be required to pay a fee of ten cents each year. When ten or more have paid their fees, the teacher will send their money to the National Association, and give the name of the Audubon Class and her own name and address. The {254} Association will then forward to the teacher for each member whose fee has been paid, the beautiful Audubon button, and a set of ten coloured pictures, together with the outline drawings and descriptive leaflets assigned to class study for that year. The teacher will also receive, free of cost, for one year, the splendid magazine Bird-Lore, which contains many valuable suggestions for teachers. It is expected that the teacher shall give at least one lesson a month on the subject of birds, for which purpose she will find the leaflets of great value as a basis for the lessons.

Rules for a Bird Study Class.--If the teacher wishes, the Audubon Class may have a regular organization, and a pupil may preside upon the occasions when the class is discussing a lesson. For this purpose the following simple constitution is suggested:

Article 1. The organization shall be known as the (give name) Junior Audubon Class.

Article 2. The object of its members shall be to learn all they can about wild birds, and to try to save any from being wantonly killed.

{255}

Article 3. The officers shall consist of a President, Secretary, and Treasurer.

Article 4. The annual fees of the class shall be 10 cents for each member; and the money shall be sent to the National Association of Audubon Societies in exchange for Educational Leaflets and Audubon Buttons.

Article 5. The Junior Audubon Class shall have at least one meeting every month.

Although most of these classes have been and will be formed among pupils in schools, any one may form a class of children anywhere, and receive the privileges offered.

Subjects for Study.--Besides the study of the particular birds in the leaflets, the following subjects may be studied with profit:

Birds' Nests.--In the fall, after all the birds have left their nests, the nests may be collected and brought to the schoolroom. Study them and learn that the Chipping Sparrow's nest is made of fine rootlets and grasses, and is lined with horsehair; {256} examine the mud cup of the Robin's nest, the soft lining of the Loggerhead Shrike's nest, etc.

Feeding Birds.--In winter arrange "bird tables" in the trees and by the windows, and place crumbs and seeds on them; in summer put out bathing and drinking pans, note what birds come to them and how frequently, and report what you observe to the class.

Nesting Boxes.--In early spring put up nesting boxes for Bluebirds, Wrens, Chickadees, Nuthatches, Martins, and other birds. The leaflets sent will be found to contain many suggestions about bird feeding and nesting boxes, and the proper way to make and place the latter.

Colouring Outlines.--The children, using crayons or water-colour paint, may place the natural colours of the birds upon the outline drawings provided, using the coloured plates for comparison. This is one of the best ways to fasten in the memory the appearance of the birds, and thus quickly learn to recognize them in the field. Many teachers have utilized this as an exercise for the regular drawing hour.

Teaching Children Approved by the Government.--Considering the importance of the subject and the success that the plan has met, it is little wonder that the Hon. P. P. Claxton, United States Commissioner of Education, early gave it his unqualified endorsement. In one letter he wrote:

"I consider the work of the Junior Audubon {258} Classes very important for both educational and economic results, and I congratulate you upon the opportunity of extending it. The bird clause in the Mosaic Law ends with the words: 'That it may be well with thee, and that thou mayest prolong thy days.' The principle still holds. I hope that through your efforts the American people may soon be better informed in regard to our wild birds and their value."

In America we have neglected the subject of protecting our bird life, and as a result in many sections we are suffering to-day from scourges of insects. Too long the careless and thoughtless have been allowed to wander aimlessly afield and shoot the birds that caused the winds of prosperity to blow. We must teach the children to avoid the errors that we have made. It is our duty to the child to give him of our best, and teach him with all his getting to get understanding.

###

www.ingramcontent.com/pod-product-compliance
Lightning Source LLC
Chambersburg PA
CBHW071054290526
45795CB00004B/1480